1989

On Metaphysics

On Metaphysics

Roderick M. Chisholm

University of Minnesota Press *Minneapolis*

Published by the University of Minnesota Press
2037 University Avenue Southeast, Minneapolis, MN 55414.
Printed in the United States of America.

Library of Congress Catalog Card Number 89-40290

ISBN 0-8166-1767-8

The author thanks the publishers of the following journals and collections for permission
to republish essays in this book. New York University Press, for Chap. 1, "Responsibility and
Avoidability," from Sidney Hook (ed.), *Determinism and Freedom in the Age of Modern
Science* (1958). Department of Philosophy, University of Kansas (Lawrence), for Chap. 2,
"Human Freedom and the Self," from *The Lindsay Lecture* (1984). *Noûs*, 1 (1967), for Chap.
3, "Identity through Possible Worlds". State University of New York Press (Albany), for
Chap. 4, "Identity through Time," from Howard E. Kiefer and Milton K. Munitz (eds.), *Language, Belief and Metaphysics* (1970). *Midwest Studies in Philosophy*, 11. (1986), for Chap.
5, "Possibility without Haecceity", D. Reidel Publishing (Dordrecht), for Chap. 6, "Coming
into Being and Passing Away: Can the Metaphysician Help?" from S. F. Spicker and H. T.
Englehardt, Jr. (eds.), *Philosophical Medical Ethics: Its Nature and Significance* (1977). *Review of Metaphysics*, 26 (1973), for Chap. 7, "Parts as Essential to their Wholes," *Grazer
Philosophische Studien*, 20 (1983), for Chap. 8, "Boundaries" (originally called "Boundaries
as Independent Particulars"), and 25/26 (1985/1986) for Chap. 16, "States and Events" (originally called "On the Positive and Negative States of Things"). MIT Press, for Chap. 9, "Scattered Objects," from Judith Jarvis Thomson (ed.), *On Being and Saying: Essays for Richard
Cartwright* (1987). *Philosophical Studies*, 43 (1983), for Chap. 10, "The Nature of the Psychological." *The Monist*, 69 (1987), for Chap. 11, "Presence in Absence." Hölder-Pichler-
Tempsky (Vienna), for Chap. 12, "Questions about Minds," which was the preface to
Proceedings of the Ninth International Wittgenstein Symposium (1985); for Chap. 15, "Properties Intentionally Considered," from *Proceedings of the Sixth International Wittgenstein
Symposium* (1982); and for Chap. 17, "The Self in Austrian Philosophy," from J. C. Nyíri
(ed.), *From Balzano to Wittgenstein: The Tradition of Austrian Philosophy* (1986). *Philosophical Exchange*, 2 (1979), for Chap. 13, "Is There a Mind-Body Problem?" *Synthèse*, 61
(1984), for Chap. 14, "The Primacy of the Intentional."

The University of Minnesota
is an equal-opportunity
educator and employer.

Contents

Introduction

Two assumptions about the nature of metaphysics are presupposed by this book. Neither is remarkable in itself. But in contemporary western philosophy each is usually associated with the rejection of the other. One assumption is that the problems of philosophy are extraordinarily difficult and can be solved only by the responsible application of what Russell called "honest toil." The other is the view of Leibniz and Brentano, according to which reflection on the self and on what it is to think provides us with the key to understanding the fundamental categories of reality.

The categories discussed here are: substance and attribute; part and whole; identity, persistence, and change; boundaries and limits; coming into being and passing away; reference and the nature of the psychological; and the self. The "intentional" approach to these topics is complemented by an "internal" approach to the theory of knowledge. The latter is exemplified by my *Foundations of Knowing* in the present series; it is further developed in the Third Edition of my *Theory of Knowledge* (Englewood Cliffs, N.J.: Prentice-Hall, 1989).

Many of the essays appear as they were originally published. Some are corrected in minor respects and certain omissions have been made. "The Primacy of the Intentional" and "States and Events" have been completely rewritten. "The Categories" is new; it was written for this book and represents a kind of *Zusammenfassung* of the ontology here set forth.

Part I
Freedom and Determinism

1

Responsibility and Avoidability

Edwards and Hospers hold that there is an important sense in which we may be said *not* to be morally responsible for any of our acts or choices. I propose the following as an explicit formulation of their reasoning:

1. If a choice is one we could not have avoided making, then it is one for which we are not morally responsible.
2. If we make a choice under conditions such that, given those conditions, it is (causally but not logically) impossible for the choice not to be made, then the choice is one we could not have avoided making.
3. Every event occurs under conditions such that, given those conditions, it is (causally but not logically) impossible for that event not to occur.
4. The making of a choice is the occurrence of an event.
∴.5. We are not morally responsible for any of our choices.

If we wish to reject the conclusion (5)—and for most of us (5) is difficult to accept—we must reject at least one of the premises.

Premise (1), I think, may be interpreted as a logical truth. If a man is responsible for what he did, then we may say, "He *could* have done otherwise." And if we may say, "He couldn't help it," then he is not responsible for what he did.

Many philosophers would deny (2), substituting a weaker account of *avoidability*. A choice is avoidable, they might say, provided only it is such that, *if* the agent had reflected further, or had reflected on certain things on which in fact he did not reflect, he would *not* have made the choice. To say of a choice that it "could *not* have been avoided," in accordance with this account, would be to say that, even if the agent *had* reflected further, on anything you like, he would all the same have made the choice. But such conditional accounts of *avoidability* ("An act or choice is avoidable provided only it is such that, *if* the agent were to do so-and-so, the act or choice would not occur") usually have this serious defect:

the antecedent clause ("if the agent were to do so-and-so") refers to some act or choice, or to the failure to perform some act or to make some choice; hence we may ask, concerning the occurrence or nonoccurrence of this act or choice, whether or not *it* is avoidable. Thus one who accepted (5) could say that, if the agent's failure to reflect further was itself unavoidable, his choice was also unavoidable. And no such conditional account of *avoidability* seems adequate to the use of "avoidable" and "unavoidable" in questions and statements such as these.

If we accept a conditional account of avoidability, we may be tempted to say, of course, that it would be a *misuse* of "avoidable" to ask whether the nonoccurrence of the antecedent event ("the agent does so-and-so") is avoidable. But the philosopher who accepts (5) may well insist that, since the antecedent clause refers to an act or a choice, the use of "avoidable" in question is *not* a misuse.

What, then, if we were to deny (3)? Suppose that some of our choices do not satisfy (3) — that when they are made they are *not* made under any conditions such that it is (causally) impossible (though logically possible) for them not to be made. If there are choices of this sort, then they are merely fortuitous or capricious. And if they are merely fortuitous or capricious, if they "just happen," then, I think, we may say with Blanshard that we are *not* morally responsible for them. Hence denying (3) is not the way to avoid (5).

We seem confronted, then, with a dilemma: either our choices have sufficient causal conditions or they do not; if they do have sufficient causal conditions they are not avoidable; if they do not, they are fortuitous or capricious; and therefore, our choices are either unavoidable or fortuitous, we are not morally responsible for them.

There are philosophers who believe that by denying the rather strange-sounding premise (4) we can escape the dilemma. Insisting on something like "the primacy of practical reason," they would say that since we are certain that (5) is false we must construct a metaphysical theory about the self, a theory denying (4) and enabling us to reconcile (3) and the denial of (5). I say "metaphysical" because it seems to be necessary for the theory to replace (4) by sentences using such terms as "active power," "the autonomy of the will," "prime mover," or "higher levels of causality" — terms designating something to which we apparently need not refer when expressing the conclusions of physics and the natural sciences. But I believe we cannot know whether such theories enable us to escape our dilemma. For it seems impossible to conceive what the relation is that, according to these theories, holds between the "will," "self," "mover," or "active power," on the one hand, and the bodily events this power is supposed to control, on the other — the relation between the "activities" of the self and the events described by physics.

I am dissatisfied, then, with what philosophers have proposed as alternatives to premises (1) through (4) above, but since I feel certain that (5) is false I also feel certain that at least one of the premises is false.

2

Human Freedom and the Self

"A staff moves a stone, and is moved by a hand, which is moved by a man."
(Aristotle, *Physics*, 256a.)

1. The metaphysical problem of human freedom might be summarized in the following way: Human beings are responsible agents; but this fact appears to conflict
with a deterministic view of human action (the view that every event that is involved in an act is caused by some other event); and it *also* appears to conflict
with an indeterministic view of human action (the view that the act, or some event
that is essential to the act, is not caused at all.) To solve the problem, I believe,
we must make somewhat far-reaching assumptions about the self or the agent —
about the man who performs the act.

Perhaps it is needless to remark that, in all likelihood, it is impossible to say
anything significant about this ancient problem that has not been said before.[1]

2. Let us consider some deed, or misdeed, that may be attributed to a responsible agent: one man, say, shot another. If the man *was* responsible for what he
did, then, I would urge, what was to happen at the time of the shooting was something that was entirely up to the man himself. There was a moment at which it
was true, both that he could have fired the shot and also that he could have
refrained from firing it. And if this is so, then, even though he did fire it, he could
have done something else instead. (He didn't find himself firing the shot 'against
his will', as we say.) I think we can say, more generally, then, that if a man is
responsible for a certain event or a certain state of affairs (in our example, the

The Lindley Lecture, 1964, pp. 3–15. © Copyright 1964 by the Department of Philosophy,
University of Kansas. Reprinted by permission of the author and of the Department of Philosophy
of the University of Kansas, Lawrence.

shooting of another man), then that event or state of affairs was brought about by some act of his, and the act was something that was in his power either to perform or not to perform.

But now if the act which he *did* perform was an act that was also in his power *not* to perform, then it could not have been caused or determined by any event that was not itself within his power either to bring about or not to bring about. For example, if what we say he did was really something that was brought about by a second man, one who forced his hand upon the trigger, say, or who, by means of hypnosis, compelled him to perform the act, then since the act was caused by the *second* man it was nothing that was within the power of the *first* man to prevent. And precisely the same thing is true, I think, if instead of referring to a second man who compelled the first one, we speak instead of the *desires* and *beliefs* which the first man happens to have had. For if what we say he did was really something that was brought about by his own beliefs and desires, if these beliefs and desires in the particular situation in which he happened to have found himself caused him to do just what it was that we say he did do, then since *they* caused it, *he* was unable to do anything other than just what it was that he did do. It makes no difference whether the cause of the deed was internal or external; if the cause was some state or event for which the man himself was not responsible, then he was not responsible for what we have been mistakenly calling his act. If a flood caused the poorly constructed dam to break, then, given the flood and the constitution of the dam, the break, we may say, *had* to occur and nothing could have happened in its place. And if the flood of desire caused the weak-willed man to give in, then he, too, had to do just what it was that he did do and he was no more responsible than was the dam for the results that followed. (It is true, of course, that if the man is responsible for the beliefs and desires that he happens to have, then he may also be responsible for the things they lead him to do. But the question now becomes: *is* he responsible for the beliefs and desires he happens to have? If he is, then there was a time when they were within his power either to acquire or not to acquire, and we are left, therefore, with our general point.)

One may object: But surely if there were such a thing as a man who is really *good*, then he would be responsible for things that he would do; yet, he would be unable to do anything other than just what it is that he does do, since, being good, he will always choose to do what is best. The answer, I think, is suggested by a comment that Thomas Reid makes on an ancient author. The author had said of Cato, 'He was good because he could not be otherwise', and Reid observes: 'This saying, if understood literally and strictly, is not the praise of Cato, but of his constitution, which was no more the work of Cato than his existence'.[2] If Cato was himself responsible for the good things that he did, then Cato, as Reid suggests, was such that, although he had the power to do what was not good, he exercised his power only for that which was good.

All of this, if it is true, may give a certain amount of comfort to those who are tender-minded. But we should remind them that it also conflicts with a familiar view about the nature of God—with the view that St. Thomas Aquinas expresses by saying that 'every movement both of the will and of nature proceeds from God as the Prime Mover'.[3] If the act of the sinner *did* proceed from God as the Prime Mover, then God was in the position of the second agent we just discussed—the man who forced the trigger finger, or the hypnotist—and the sinner, so-called, was *not* responsible for what he did. (This may be a bold assertion, in view of the history of western theology, but I must say that I have never encountered a single good reason for denying it.)

There is one standard objection to all of this and we should consider it briefly.

3. The objection takes the form of a stratagem—one designed to show that determinism (and divine providence) is consistent with human responsibility. The stratagem is one that was used by Jonathan Edwards and by many philosophers in the present century, most notably, G. E. Moore.[4]

One proceeds as follows: The expression

(a) He could have done otherwise,

it is argued, means no more nor less than

(b) If he had chosen to do otherwise, then he would have done otherwise.

(In place of 'chosen', one might say 'tried', 'set out', 'decided', 'undertaken', or 'willed'.) The truth of statement (b), it is then pointed out, is consistent with determinism (and with divine providence); for even if all of the man's actions were causally determined, the man could still be such that, *if* he had chosen otherwise, then he would have done otherwise. What the murderer saw, let us suppose, along with his beliefs and desires, *caused* him to fire the shot; yet he was such that *if*, just then, he had chosen or decided *not* to fire the shot, then he would not have fired it. All of this is certainly possible. Similarly, we could say, of the dam, that the flood caused it to break and also that the dam was such that, *if* there had been no flood or any similar pressure, then the dam would have remained intact. And therefore, the argument proceeds, if (b) is consistent with determinism, and if (a) and (b) say the same thing, then (a) is also consistent with determinism; hence we can say that the agent *could* have done otherwise even though he was caused to do what he did do; and therefore determinism and moral responsibility are compatible.

Is the argument sound? The conclusion follows from the premises, but the catch, I think, lies in the first premiss—the one saying that statement (a) tells us no more nor less than what statement (b) tells us. For (b), it would seem, could be true while (a) is false. That is to say, our man might be such that, if he had chosen to do otherwise, then he would have done otherwise, and yet *also* such that he could not have done otherwise. Suppose, after all, that our murderer could not have *chosen*, or could not have *decided*, to do otherwise. Then the fact that he happens also to be a man such that, if he had chosen not to shoot he would not have shot, would make no difference. For if he could *not* have chosen *not* to shoot, then he could not have done anything other than just what it was that he did do. In a word: from our statement (b) above ('If he had chosen to do otherwise, then he would have done otherwise'), we cannot make an inference to (a) above ('He could have done otherwise') unless we can *also* assert:

(c) He could have chosen to do otherwise.

And therefore, if we must reject this third statement (c), then, even though we may be justified in asserting (b), we are not justified in asserting (a). If the man could not have chosen to do otherwise, then he would not have done otherwise — *even if* he was such that, if he *had* chosen to do otherwise, then he would have done otherwise.

The stratagem in question, then, seems to me not to work, and I would say, therefore, that the ascription of responsibility conflicts with a deterministic view of action.

4. Perhaps there is less need to argue that the ascription of responsibility also conflicts with an indeterministic view of action — with the view that the act, or some event that is essential to the act, is not caused at all. If the act — the firing of the shot — was not caused at all, if it was fortuitous or capricious, happening so to speak out of the blue, then, presumably, no one — and nothing — was responsible for the act. Our conception of action, therefore, should be neither deterministic nor indeterministic. Is there any other possibility?

5. We must not say that every event involved in the act is caused by some other event; and we must not say that the act is something that is not caused at all. The possibility that remains, therefore, is this: We should say that at least one of the events that are involved in the act is caused, not by any other events, but by something else instead. And this something else can only be the agent — the man. If there is an event that is caused, not by other events, but by the man, then there are some events involved in the act that are not caused by other events. But if the event in question is caused by the man then it *is* caused and we are not committed to saying that there is something involved in the act that is not caused at all.

But this, of course, is a large consequence, implying something of considerable importance about the nature of the agent or the man.

6. If we consider only inanimate natural objects, we may say that causation, if it occurs, is a relation between *events* or *states of affairs*. The dam's breaking was an event that was caused by a set of other events — the dam being weak, the flood being strong, and so on. But if a man is responsible for a particular deed, then, if what I have said is true, there is some event, or set of events, that is caused, *not* by other events or states of affairs, but by the agent, whatever he may be.

I shall borrow a pair of medieval terms, using them, perhaps, in a way that is slightly different from that for which they were originally intended. I shall say that when one event or state of affairs (or set of events or states of affairs) causes some other event or state of affairs, then we have an instance of *transeunt* causation. And I shall say that when an *agent*, as distinguished from an event, causes an event or state of affairs, then we have an instance of *immanent* causation.

The nature of what is intended by the expression 'immanent causation' may be illustrated by this sentence from Aristotle's *physics:* "Thus, a staff moves a stone, and is moved by a hand, which is moved by a man" (VII, 5, 256a, 6–8). If the man was responsible, then we have in this illustration a number of instances of causation—most of them transeunt but at least one of them immanent. What the staff did to the stone was an instance of transeunt causation, and thus we may describe it as a relation between events: "the motion of the staff caused the motion of the stone." And similarly for what the hand did to the staff: "the motion of the hand caused the motion of the staff." And, as we know from physiology, there are still other events which caused the motion of the hand. Hence we need not introduce the agent at this particular point, as Aristotle does—we *need* not, though we *may*. We *may* say that the hand was moved by the man, but we may *also* say that the motion of the hand was caused by the motion of certain muscles; and we may say that the motion of the muscles was caused by certain events that took place within the brain. But some event, and presumably one of those that took place within the brain, was caused by the agent and not by any other events.

There are, of course, objections to this way of putting the matter; I shall consider the two that seem to me to be most important.

7. One may object, firstly: "If the *man* does anything, then, as Aristotle's remark suggests, what he does is to move the *hand*. But he certainly does not *do* anything to his brain—he may not even know that he *has* a brain. And if he doesn't do anything to the brain, and if the motion of the hand was caused by something that happened within the brain, then there is no point in appealing to 'immanent causation' as being something incompatible with 'transeunt causation'—for the whole thing, after all, is a matter of causal relations among events or states of affairs."

The answer to this objection, I think, is this: It is true that the agent does not *do* anything with his brain, or to his brain, in the sense in which he *does* something with his hand and does something to the staff. But from this it does not follow that the agent was not the immanent cause of something that happened within his brain.

We should note a useful distinction that has been proposed by Professor A. I. Melden—namely, the distinction between 'making something A happen' and 'doing A'.[5] If I reach for the staff and pick it up, then one of the things that I *do* is just that—reach for the staff and pick it up. And if it is something that I do, then there is a very clear sense in which it may be said to be something that I know that I do. If you ask me, "Are you doing something, or trying to do something, with the staff?", I will have no difficulty in finding an answer. But in doing something with the staff, I also make various things happen which are not in this same sense things that I do: I will make various air-particles move; I will free a number of blades of grass from the pressure that had been upon them; and I may cause a shadow to move from one place to another. If these are merely things that I make happen, as distinguished from things that I do, then I may know nothing whatever about them; I may not have the slightest idea that, in moving the staff, I am bringing about any such thing as the motion of air-particles, shadows, and blades of grass.

We may say, in answer to the first objection, therefore, that it is true that our agent does nothing to his brain or with his brain; but from this it does not follow that the agent is not the immanent cause of some event within his brain; for the brain event may be something which, like the motion of the air-particles, he made happen in picking up the staff. The only difference between the two cases is this: in each case, he made something happen when he picked up the staff; but in the one case — the motion of the air particles or of the shadows — it was the motion of the staff that caused the event to happen; and in the other case — the event that took place in the brain — it was this event that caused the motion of the staff.

The point is, in a word, that whenever a man does something A, then (by 'immanent causation') he makes a certain cerebral event happen, and this cerebral event (by 'transeunt causation') makes A happen.

8. The second objection is more difficult and concerns the very concept of 'immanent causation', or causation by an agent, as this concept is to be interpreted here. The concept is subject to a difficulty which has long been associated with that of the prime mover removed. We have said that there must be some event A, presumably some cerebral event, which is caused not by an other event, but by the agent. Since A was not caused by any other event, then the agent himself cannot be said to have undergone any change or produced any other event (such as 'an act of will' or the like) which brought A about. But if, when the agent made A happen, there was no event involved other than A itself, no event which could be described as *making* A happen, what did the agent's causation consist of? What, for example, is the difference between A's just happening, and the agent's *causing* A to happen? We cannot attribute the difference to any event that took place within the agent. And so far as the event A itself is concerned, there would seem to be no discernible difference. Thus Aristotle said that the activity of the prime mover is nothing in addition to the motion that it produces, and Suarez said that 'the action is in reality nothing but the effect as it flows from the agent'.[6] Must we conclude, then, that there is no more to the man's action in causing event A than there is to the event A's happening by itself? Here we would seem to have a distinction without a difference — in which case we have failed to find a *via media* between a deterministic and an indeterministic view of action.

The only answer, I think, can be this: that the difference between the man's causing A, on the one hand, and the event A just happening, on the other, lies in the fact that, in the first case but not the second, the event A *was* caused and was caused by the man. There was a brain event A; the agent did, in fact, cause the brain event; but there was nothing that he did to cause it.

This answer may not entirely satisfy and it will be likely to provoke the following question: 'But what are you really *adding* to the assertion that A happened when you utter the words "The agent *caused* A to happen"?' As soon as we have put the question this way, we see, I think, that whatever difficulty we may have encountered is one that may be traced to the concept of causation generally — whether 'immanent' or 'transeunt'. The problem, in other words, is not a problem that is peculiar to our conception of human action. It is a problem that must be faced by anyone who makes use of the concept of causation at all; and therefore, I would say, it is a problem for everyone but the complete indeterminist.

For the problem, as we put it, referring just to 'immanent causation', or causation by an agent, was this: 'What is the difference between saying, of an event A, that A just happened and saying that someone caused A to happen?' The analogous problem, which holds for 'transeunt causation', or causation by an event, is this: 'What is the difference between saying, of two events A and B, that B happened and then A happened, and saying that B's happening was the *cause* of A's happening?' And the only answer that one can give is this — that in the one case the agent was the cause of A's happening and in the other case event B was the cause of A's happening. The nature of transeunt causation is no more clear than is that of immanent causation.

9. But we may plausibly say — and there is a respectable philosophical tradition to which we may appeal — that the notion of immanent causation; or causation by an agent, is in fact more clear than that of transeunt causation, or causation by an event, and that it is only by understanding our own causal efficacy, as agents, that we can grasp the concept of *cause* at all. Hume may be said to have shown that we do not derive the concept of *cause* from what we perceive of external things. How, then, do we derive it? The most plausible suggestion, it seems to me, is that of Reid, once again: namely that 'the conception of an efficient cause may very probably be derived from the experience we have had . . . of our own power to produce certain effects'.[7] If we did not understand the concept of immanent causation, we would not understand that of transeunt causation.

10. It may have been noted that I have avoided the term 'free will' in all of this. For even if there is such a faculty as 'the will', which somehow sets our acts agoing, the question of freedom, as John Locke said, is not the question "*whether the will be free*"; it is the question "*whether a man be free.*"[8] For if there is a 'will', as a moving faculty, the question is whether the man is free to will to do these things that he does will to do — and also whether he is free *not* to will any of those things that he does will to do, and, again, whether he is free to will any of those things that he does not will to do. Jonathan Edwards tried to restrict himself to the question — "Is the man free to do what it is that he wills?" — but the answer to this question will not tell us whether the man is responsible for what it is that he

does will to do. Using still another pair of medieval terms, we may say that the metaphysical problem of freedom does not concern the *actus imperatus*; it does not concern the question whether we are free to accomplish whatever it is that we will or set out to do; it concerns the *actus elicitus*, the question whether we are free to will or to set out to do those things that we do will or set out to do.

11. If we are responsible, and if what I have been trying to say is true, then we have a prerogative which some would attribute only to God: each of us, when we act, is a prime mover unmoved. In doing what we do, we cause certain events to happen, and nothing — or no one — causes us to cause those events to happen.

12. If we are thus prime movers unmoved and if our actions, or those for which we are responsible, are not causally determined, then they are not causally determined by our *desires*. And this means that the relation between what we want or what we desire, on the one hand, and what it is that we do, on the other, is not as simple as most philosophers would have it.

We may distinguish between what we might call the 'Hobbist approach' and what we might call the 'Kantian approach' to this question. The Hobbist approach is the one that is generally accepted at the present time, but the Kantian approach, I believe, is the one that is true. According to Hobbism, if we *know*, of some man, what his beliefs and desires happen to he and how strong they are, if we know what he feels certain of, what he desires more than anything else, and if we know the state of his body and what stimuli he is being subjected to, then we may *deduce*, logically, just what it is that he will do — or, more accurately, just what it is that he will try, set out, or undertake to do. Thus Professor Melden has said that "the connection between wanting and doing is logical."[9] But according to the Kantian approach to our problem, and this is the one that I would take, there is no such logical connection between wanting and doing, nor need there even be a causal connection. No set of statements about a man's desires, beliefs, and stimulus situation at any time implies any statement telling us what the man will try, set out, or undertake to do at that time. As Reid put it, though we may 'reason from men's motives to their actions and, in many cases, with great probability', we can never do so 'with absolute certainty'.[10]

This means that, in one very strict sense of the terms, there can be no science of man. If we think of science as a matter of finding out what laws happen to hold, and if the statement of a law tells us what kinds of events are caused by what other kinds of events, then there will be human actions which we cannot explain by subsuming them under any laws. We cannot say, 'It is causally necessary that, given such and such desires and beliefs, and being subject to such and such stimuli, the agent will do so and so'. For at times the agent, if he chooses, may rise above his desires and do something else instead.

But all of this is consistent with saying that, perhaps more often than not, our desires do exist under conditions such that those conditions necessitate us to act.

And we may also say, with Leibniz, that at other times our desires may 'incline without necessitating'.

13. Leibniz's phrase presents us with our final philosophical problem. What does it mean to say that a desire, or a motive, might "incline without necessitating"? There is a temptation, certainly, to say that "to incline" means to cause and that "not to necessitate" means not to cause, but obviously we cannot have it both ways.

Nor will Leibniz's own solution do. In his letter to Coste, he puts the problem as follows: "When a choice is proposed, for example to go out or not to go out, it is a question whether, with all the circumstances, internal and external, motives, perceptions, dispositions, impressions, passions, inclinations taken together, I am still in a contingent state, or whether I am necessitated to make the choice, for example, to go out; that is to say, whether this proposition true and determined in fact, *In all these circumstances taken together I shall choose to go out*, is contingent or necessary."[11] Leibniz's answer might be put us follows: in one sense of the terms "necessary" and "contingent", the proposition "In all these circumstances taken together I shall choose to go out," may be said to be contingent and not necessary, and in another sense of these terms, it may be said to be necessary and not contingent. But the sense in which the proposition may be said to be contingent, according to Leibniz, is only this: there is no logical contradiction involved in denying the proposition. And the sense in which it may be said to be necessary is this: since "nothing ever occurs without cause or determining reason'," the proposition is causally necessary. "Whenever all the circumstances taken together are such that the balance of deliberation is heavier on one side than on the other, it is certain and infallible that that is the side that is going to win out." But if what we have been saying is true, the proposition 'In all these circumstances taken together I shall choose to go out', may be causally as well as logically contingent. Hence we must find another interpretation for Leibniz's statement that our motives and desires may incline us, or influence us, to choose without thereby necessitating us to choose.

Let us consider a public official who has some moral scruples but who also, as one says, could be had. Because of the scruples that he does have, he would never take any positive steps receive a bribe—he would not actively solicit one. But his morality has its limits and he is also such that, if we were to confront him with a *fait accompli* or to let him see what is about to happen ($10,000 in cash is being deposited behind the garage), then he would succumb and be unable to resist. The general situation is a familiar one and this is one reason that people pray to be delivered from temptation. (It also justifies Kant's remark: "And how many there are who may have led a long blameless life, who are only *fortunate* in having escaped so many temptations."[12] Our relation to the misdeed that we contemplate may not be a matter simply of being able to bring it about or not to bring it about. As St. Anselm noted, there are at least four possibilities. We may illustrate them by reference to our public official and the event which is his receiving the bribe, in the following way: (i) he may be able to bring the event about himself (*facere esse*), in which case he would actively cause himself to receive the bribe; (ii) he may be able to refrain from bringing it about himself (*non facere esse*), in which case he would not himself do anything to insure that he receive the bribe; (iii) he may be able to do something to prevent the event from occurring (*facere non esse*), in which case he would make sure that the $10,000 was *not* left behind the garage; or (iv) he may be unable to do anything to prevent the event from occuring (*non facere non esse*), in which case, though he may not solicit the bribe, he would allow himself to keep it.[13] We have envisaged our official as a man who can resist the temptation to (i) but cannot resist the temptation to (iv): he can refrain from bringing the event about himself, but he cannot bring himself to do anything to prevent it.

Let us think of 'inclination without necessitation', then, in such terms as these. First we may contrast the two propositions:

(1) He can resist the temptation to do something in order to make A happen;

(2) He can resist the temptation to allow A to happen (i.e. to do nothing to prevent A from happening).

We may suppose that the man has some desire to have A happen and thus has a motive for making A happen. His motive for making A happen, I suggest, is one that *necessitates* provided that, because of the motive, (1) is false; he cannot resist the temptation to do something in order to make A happen. His motive for making A happen is one that *inclines* provided that, because of the motive, (2) is false; like our public official, he cannot bring himself to do anything to prevent A from happening. And therefore we can say that this motive for making A happen is one that *inclines but does not necessitate* provided that, because of the motive, (1) is true and (2) is false; he can resist the temptation to make it happen but he cannot resist the temptation to allow it to happen.

Notes

1. The general position to be presented here is suggested in the following writings, among others: Aristotle, *Eudemian Ethics*, Book II, Chap. 6; *Nicomachean Ethics*, Book III, Chaps. 1–5; Thomas Reid, *Essays on the Active Powers of Man*; C. A. Campbell, "Is 'Free Will' a Pseudo-Problem?" *Mind*, N.S. 60 (1951): 441–65; Roderick M. Chisholm, "Responsibility and Avoidability," and Richard Taylor, "Determination and the Theory of Agency," in Sidney Hook (ed.), *Determinism and Freedom in the Age of Modern Science* (New York: New York University Press, 1958).

2. Thomas Reid, *Essays on the Active Powers of Man*, Essay IV, Chap. 4 (*Works*, P. 600).

3. *Summa Theologia*, First Part of the Second Part, Question VI ("On the Voluntary and Involuntary").

4. Jonathan Edwards, *Freedom of the Will* (New Haven, Conn.: Yale University Press, 1957); G. E. Moore, *Ethics* (Home University Library, 1912), Chap. 6.

5. A. I. Melden, *Free Action* (Oxford: Basil Blackwell, 1961), especially Chap. 3. Mr. Melden's own views, however, are quite the contrary of those proposed here.

6. Aristotle, *Physics*, Book III, Chap. 3; Suarez, *Disputationes Metaphysicae*, Disputation 18, Sec. 10.

7. Reid, *Works*, p. 524.

8. *Essay Concerning Human Understanding*, Book II, Chap. 21.

9. Melden, *Free Action*, p. 166.

10. Reid, *Works*, pp. 608, 612.

11. "Lettre à Mr. Coste de la Nécessité et de la Contingence" (1707), in Johanne E. Erdmann (ed.), *Opera Philosophica* (Berlin: Sumtibus G. Eichleri, 1840), pp. 447–49.

12. In the preface to the *Metaphysical Elements of Ethics*, in T. K. Abbot (ed.), *Kant's Critique of Practical Reason and Other Works on the Theory of Ethics* (London: Longman's Green, 1959), p. 303.

13. Cf. D. P. Henry, "Saint Anselm's De 'Grammatico'," *Philosophical Quarterly*, 10 (1960): 115–26. St. Anselm noted that (i) and (iii), respectively, may be thought of as forming the upper left and the upper right corners of a square of opposition, and (ii) and (iv) the lower right and the lower left.

Part II
Coming into Being, Persisting, and Passing Away

3

Identity through Possible Worlds

> It is now easy to see a simple way of avoiding undesirable existential generalizations in epistemic contexts. Existential generalization with respect to a term – say b – is admissible in such contexts if b refers to one and the same man in all the "possible worlds" we have to consider.[1]

In an article on Hintikka's *Knowledge and Belief*, I suggested that certain difficult questions come to mind when we consider the thought that an individual in one possible world might be identical with an individual in another possible world.[2] The present paper is written in response to the editor's invitation to be more explicit about these questions.

Let us suppose, then, that the figure of an infinity of possible worlds makes good sense and let us also suppose, for simplicity of presentation, that we have a complete description of this one. We may consider some one of the entities of this world, alter its description slightly, adjust the descriptions of the other entities in the world to fit this alteration, and then ask ourselves whether the entity in the possible world that we thus arrive at is identical with the entity we started with in this world. We start with Adam, say; we alter his description slightly and allow him to live for 931 years instead of for only 930; we then accommodate our descriptions of the other entities of the world to fit this possibility (Eve, for example, will now have the property of being married to a man who lives for 931 years instead of that of being married to a man who lives for only 930); and we thus arrive at a description of another possible world.[3]

Let us call our present world "W^1" and the possible world we have just indicated "W^2". Is the Adam of our world W^1 the same person as the Adam of the possible world W^2? In other words, is Adam such that he lives for just 930 years in W^1 and for 931 in W^2? And how are we to decide?

One's first thought might be that the proposition that Adam is in both worlds is incompatible with the principle of the indiscernibility of identicals. How could our Adam be identical with that one of ours lives for just 930 years and that one for 931? Possibly this question could be answered in the following way:

"Compare the question: How can Adam at the age of 930 be the same person as the man who ate the forbidden fruit, if the former is old and the latter is young? Here the proper reply would be: it is not true that the old Adam has properties that render him discernible from the young Adam; the truth is, rather, that Adam has the property of being young when he eats the forbidden fruit and the property of being old in the year 930, and that these properties, though different, are not incompatible. And so, too, for the different possible worlds: It is not true that the Adam of W^1 has properties that render him discernible from the Adam of W^2; the truth is, rather, that Adam has the property of living for 930 years in W^1 and the property of living for 931 in W^2, and that these properties, though different, are not incompatible."

I think it is clear that we must deal with the old Adam and the young Adam in the manner indicated; but in this case, one could argue, we know independently that the same Adam is involved throughout. But are we justified in dealing in a similar way with the Adam of W^1 and the Adam of W^2? In this latter case, one might say, we do not know independently that the same Adam is involved throughout. Here, then, is one of the questions that I do not know how to answer. Let us suppose, however, that we answer it affirmatively.

The Adam of this world, we are assuming, is identical with the Adam of that one. In other words, Adam is such that he lives for only 930 years in W^1 and for 931 in W^2. Let us now suppose further that we have arrived at our conception of W^2, not only by introducing alterations in our description of the Adam of W^1, but also by introducing alterations in our description of the Noah of W^1. We say; "Suppose Adam had lived for 931 years instead of 930 and suppose Noah had lived for 949 years instead of 950." We then arrive at our description of W^2 by accommodating our descriptions of the other entities of W^1 in such a way that these entities will be capable of inhabiting the same possible world as the revised Noah and the revised Adam. Both Noah and Adam, then, may be found in W^2 as well as in W^1.

Now let us move from W^2 to still another possible world W^3. Once again, we will start by introducing alterations in Adam and Noah and then accommodate the rest of the world to what we have done. In W^3 Adam lives for 932 years and Noah for 948. Then moving from one possible world to another, but keeping our fingers, so to speak, on the same two entities, we arrive at a world in which Noah lives for 930 years and Adam for 950. In that world, therefore, Noah has the age that Adam has in this one, and Adam has the age that Noah has in this one; the Adam and Noah that we started with might thus be said to have exchanged their ages. Now let us continue on to still other possible worlds and allow them to exchange still other properties. We will imagine a possible world in which they have exchanged the first letters of their names, then one in which they have exchanged the second, then one in which they have exchanged the fourth, with the result that

Adam in this new possible world will be called "Noah" and Noah "Adam." Proceeding in this way, we arrive finally at a possible world W^n which would seem to be exactly like our present world W^1, except for the fact that the Adam of W^n may be traced back to the Noah of W^1 and the Noah of W^n may be traced back to the Adam of W^1.

Should we say of the Adam of W^n that he is identical with the Noah of W^1 and should we say of the Noah of W^n that he is identical the Adam of W^1? In other words, is there an x such that x is Adam in W^1 and x is Noah in W^n, and is there a y such that y is Noah in W^1 and y is Adam in W^n? And how are we to decide?

But let us suppose that somehow we have arrived at an affirmative answer. Now we must ask ourselves: How is one to tell the difference between the two worlds W^1 and W^n? Shall we say that, though they are diverse, they are yet indiscernible from each other — or, at any rate, that the Adam of W^1 is indiscernible from the Adam of W^n (who is in fact the Noah of W^1) and that the Noah of W^1 is indiscernible from the Noah of W^n (who is in fact the Adam of W^1)? There is a certain ambiguity in "discernible" and in "indiscernible." The two Adams could be called "discernible" in that the one has the property of being Noah in the other world and the other does not, and similarly for the two Noahs. But in the sense of "indiscernible" that allows us to say that "Indiscernibles are identical" tells us more than merely "Identicals are identical," aren't the two Adams, the two Noahs, and the two worlds indiscernible? Could God possibly have had a sufficient reason for creating W^1 instead of W^n?

If W^1 and W^n are two different possible worlds, then, of course, there are indefinitely many others, equally difficult to distinguish from each other and from W^1 and W^n. For what we have done to Adam and Noah, we can do to any other pair of entities. Therefore among the possible worlds that would seem to be indiscernible from this one, there are those in which you play the role that I play in this one and in which I play the role that you play in this one.[4] (If this is true, there may be good ground for the existentialist's *Angst*; since, it would seem, God could have had no sufficient reason for choosing the world in which you play your present role instead of one in which you play mine.)

Is there really a good reason for saying that this Adam and Noah are identical, respectively, with that Noah and Adam? We opened the door to this conclusion by assuming that Adam could be found in more than one possible world — by assuming that there is an x such that x is Adam in W^1 and lives here for 930 years and x is also Adam in W^2 and lives there for 931. If it is reasonable to assume that Adam retains his identity through the relatively slight changes involved in the transition from W^1 to W^2, and so, too, for Noah, then it would also seem reasonable to assume that each retains his identity through the equally slight changes involved in all the other transitions that took us finally to W^n. (These transitions, of course, may be as gradual as one pleases. Instead of it being a year that we take away from Noah in our first step and give to Adam, it could be only a day, or a fraction of a second.) But identity is transitive. And therefore, one might argue, once we allow Adam to exist in more than one possible world, we commit ourselves to affirmative answers to the puzzling questions we have encountered.

Is there a way, then, in which we might reasonably countenance identity through possible worlds and yet avoid such extreme conclusions? The only way, so far as I can see, is to appeal to some version of the doctrine that individual things have essential properties. One possibility would be this:

For every entity x, there are certain properties N and certain properties E such that: x has N in some possible worlds and x has non-N in others; but x has E in every possible world in which x exists; and, moreover, for every y, if y has E in any possible world, then y is identical with x. (If "being identical with x" refers to a property of x, then we should add that E includes certain properties other than that of being identical with x.) The properties E will thus be *essential* to x and the properties N *nonessential*, or accidental.[5]

To avoid misunderstanding, we should contrast this present use of "essential property" with two others.

(1) Sometimes the "essential properties" of a thing are said to be just those properties that the thing has *necessarily*. But it is not implausible to say that there are certain properties which are such that *everything* has those properties necessarily; the properties, the example, of being either red or non-red, of being colored if red, and of being self-identical.[6] Thus the Eiffel Tower is necessarily red or non-red, necessarily colored if red, and necessarily self-identical; and so is everything else.[7]

(2) And sometimes it is said (most unfortunately, it seems to me) that each individual thing is such that it has certain properties that are essential or necessary to it "under certain descriptions of it" and that are not essential or necessary to it "under certain other descriptions of it." Thus "under one of his descriptions," the property of being President is said to be essential to Mr. Johnson whereas "under that description" the property of being the husband of Lady Bird is not; and "under another one of his descriptions," it is the other way around. Presumably *every* property P of every individual thing x is such that, "under some description of x," P is essential or necessary to x.

But if E is the set of properties that are essential to a given thing x, in the sense of "essential" that we have defined above, then: E will not be a universal property (indeed, *nothing* but x will have E); some of the properties of x will not be included in E; and E will not be such that there are descriptions of x "under which" E is not, in the sense defined, essential to x.

If we accept this doctrine of essential properties, we may say, perhaps, that the property of living for just 930 years is essential to Adam and therefore that he may inhabit other possible worlds without living for just 930 years in each of them. And so, too, perhaps, for having a name which, in English, ends with the letter "m". But, we may then go on to say, somewhere in the journey from W^1 to W^n, we left the essential properties of Adam (and therefore Adam himself) behind. But where? What *are* the properties that are essential to Adam? Being the first man? Having a name which, in English, begins with the first letter of the alphabet? But why *these* properties? If we can contemplate Adam with slightly different properties in another possible world, why can't we think of him as having ancestors in some possible worlds and as having a different name in others? And similarly for any other property that might be proposed as being thus essential to Adam.

It seems to me that even if Adam does have such essential properties, there is no procedure at all for finding out what they are. And it also seems to me that there is no way of finding out whether he *does* have any essential properties. Is there really a good reason, then, for supposing that he does?

The distinction between essential and non-essential properties seems to be involved in one of the traditional ways of dealing with the problem of *knowing who*.[8] If this way of dealing with that problem were satisfactory, then the doctrine of essential properties might have a kind of independent confirmation. But I am not sure that is satisfactory. The problem of *knowing who* may be illustrated in this way. I do not know who it was who robbed the bank this morning, but I do know, let us assume, that there is someone who robbed the bank and I also know that that person is the man who drove off from the bank at 9:20 A.M. in a Buick Sedan. For me to know *who* he is, therefore, it is not enough for me to have information enabling me to characterize him uniquely. What kind of information, then, *would* entitle me to say that I know who he is? The essentialistic answer would be: "You *know who* the bank robber is, provided that there is a certain set of properties E which are essential to the x such that x robbed the bank and you know that x has E and x robbed the bank." But if my doubts about essential properties are well-founded, this solution to the problem of knowing who would imply that the police, though they may finally "learn the thief's identity," will never know that they do. For to *know that one knows who* the thief is (according to the proposed solution) one must know what properties are essential to the thief; and if what I have said is correct, we have no way of finding out what they are. How are the police to decide that they know who the thief is if they have no answer to the metaphysical question "What are the essential properties of the man we have arrested?"[9]

It is assumed, in many writings on modal logic, that "Necessarily, for every x, x is identical with x" implies "For every x, necessarily x is identical with x," and therefore also "For every x and y, if x is identical with y, then necessarily x is identical with y." But is the assumption reasonable? It leads us to perplexing conclusions: for example, to the conclusion that *every* entity exists in *every* possible world and therefore, presumably, that everything is an *ens necessarium*.

Why assume that necessarily the evening star is identical with the evening star? We should remind ourselves that "The evening star is identical with the evening star" is not a logical truth, for it implies the contingent proposition "There is an evening star," and that its negation is not "The evening star is diverse from the evening star." Wouldn't it be simpler to deny that "Necessarily, for every x, x is identical with x" implies "For every x, necessarily x is identical with x"? Then we could deny the principle *de dicto*, "Necessarily the evening star is identical with the evening star," and also deny the principle, *de re*, "The evening star is necessarily identical with the evening star."[10] We could still do justice to the necessity that is here involved, it seems to me, provided we continued to affirm such principles, *de dicto*, as "Necessarily, for every x, x is identical with x" and "Necessarily, for every x and y, if x is identical with y then y is identical with x," and such principles, *de re*, "The evening star, like everything else, is necessarily self-identical."

Notes

1. Jaakko Hintikka, *Knowledge and Belief: An Introduction to the Logic of the Two Notions* (Ithaca, N.Y.: Cornell University Press, 1962), p. 152.

2. "The Logic of Knowing," *Journal of Philosophy*, 60 (1963): 773–95; see esp. 787–95.

3. It should be noted that the possible world in question is not one that Hintikka would call *epistemically* possible, for it could be said to contain certain states of affairs (Adam living for 931 years) that are incompatible with what we know to hold of this world; hence it is not one of the worlds Hintikka is concerned with in the passage quoted above. But it is *logically* possible, and that is all that matters for purposes of the present discussion.

4. "She (Ivich) looked at the glass, and Mathieu looked at her. A violent and undefined desire had taken possession of him; a desire to *be* for one instant that unconsciousness . . . to feel those long slender arms from within. . . . To be Ivich and not to cease to be himself." Sartre, *The Age of Reason*. Compare N. L. Wilson, "Substance without Substrata," *Review of Metaphysics*, 12 (1959), and A. N. Prior, "Identifiable Individuals," *Review of Metaphysics*, 13 (1960).

5. We could put the doctrine more cautiously by saying that the distinction between the two types of property holds, not for *every* entity x, but only for *some* entities x. But what reason could there be for thinking that it holds of some entities and not of others?

6. Sometimes these properties are called "analytic properties" or "tautological properties"; but the property of being colored if red should not be so-called if, as some have argued, "Everything that is red is colored" is not analytic.

7. From the proposition that the Eiffel Tower is red and necessarily colored if red, it would be fallacious to infer that the Eiffel Tower is necessarily colored; this is the fallacy of inferring *necessitate consequentis* from *necessitate consequentiae*. And from the proposition that the Eiffel Tower is necessarily red or non-red, it would be fallacious to infer that the proposition that the Eiffel Tower is red or non-red is a necessary proposition; the proposition could hardly be necessary, for it implies the contingent proposition that there is an Eiffel Tower. This latter fallacy might be called the fallacy of inferring *necessitate de dicto* from *necessitate de re*.

8. Compare Aristotle, *De Sophisticis Elenchis*, 179 b 3; Petrus Hispanus *Summulae Logicales*, ed. I. M. Bochenski (Turin: La Scuola, 1947), 7.41; Franz Brentano, *Kategorienlehre* (Leipzig: Felix Meiner Verlag, 1933), p. 165.

9. Hintikka says that we know who the thief is provided that there exists an x such that we know that the thief is identical with x (*Knowledge and Belief*, p. 153). But under what conditions may it be said that there exists an x such that we know that the thief is identical with x? Presumably, if ever, when we catch him in the act—when we *see* him steal the money. But the teller saw him steal the money and *she* doesn't know who he is. I have suggested elsewhere a slightly different way of looking at these questions; compare "Believing and Intentionality," *Philosophy and Phenomenological Research*, 25 (1964): 266–69, esp. 268.

10. I have discussed this possibility in "Query on Substitutivity," in Robert S. Cohen and Marx W. Wartofsky (eds.), *Boston Studies in the Philosophy of Science*, vol. 2 (New York: The Humanities Press, 1965), pp. 275–78.

If we deny that "Necessarily, for every x, x is F" implies "For every x, necessarily x is F," then presumably we should also deny that "It is possible that there exists an x such that x is F" implies "There exists an x such that it is possible that x is F." But isn't this what we should do? One could hold quite consistently, it seems to me, that though it is possible that there exists something having the properties that Christians attribute to God, yet nothing that does exist is such that it is possible that *that* thing has the properties that Christians attribute to God.

4

Identity through Time

According to Bishop Butler, when we say of a physical thing existing at one time that it is identical with or the same as a physical thing existing at some other time ("this is the same ship we traveled on before"), we are likely to be using the expression "same" or "identical" in a "loose and popular sense." But when we say of a person existing at one time that he is identical with or the same as a person existing at some other time ("the ship has the same captain it had before"), we are likely to be using "same" or "identical" in a "strict and philosophical sense."[1] I shall attempt to give an interpretation to these two theses; and I shall suggest that there is at least an element of truth in each.

To illustrate the first of the two theses—that it is likely to be only in a loose and popular sense that we may speak of the identity of a physical thing through time—let us recall the traditional problem of the ship of Theseus, in a somewhat updated version. The ship, when it came to be, was made entirely of wood. One day a wooden plank was replaced by an aluminum one (this is the updating) and the wooden plank was cast off. But we still had the same ship, it was said, since the change was only slight. Somewhat later, another wooden plank was cast off and also replaced by an aluminum one. Still the same ship, of course, since, once again, the change was only slight. The changes continue, but they are always sufficiently slight so that the ship on any given day can be said to be the same as the ship on the day before. Finally, of course, the ship is made entirely of aluminum. Some will feel certain that the aluminum ship is the same ship as the one that was once made entirely of wood. After all, it preserved its identity from one change to the next, and identity is transitive. Consider, however, this possibility, suggested by Thomas Hobbes: " . . . if some man had kept the old planks as they were taken out, and by putting them afterwards together in the same order, had again made a ship of them, this, without doubt, had also been the same numerical ship with that which was at the beginning; and so there would have been two

25

ships numerically the same, which is absurd."[2] To compound the problem, let us imagine that the captain of the original ship had taken a vow to the effect that if his ship were ever to go down, then he would go down with it. What now, if the two ships collide at sea and he sees them start to sink together? Where does his duty lie—with the aluminum ship or with the reassembled wooden ship?

Putting the problem schematically, we may suppose that on Monday a simple ship, "The U.S.S. *South Dakota*," came into being, composed of two principle parts, *A* and *B*. On Tuesday, part *A* is replaced by a new part *C*. (We may imagine that the replacement was accomplished with a minimum of disturbance: as *A* was eased off, *C* was pushed on immediately behind and in such a way that one could not say at any time during the process that there was only half a ship in the harbor.) On Wednesday, there was fission, with *B* going off to the left and annexing itself to *F* as it departed from *C*, and with *C* going off to the right and annexing itself to *J* as it departed from *B*. On Thursday, over at the left, *B* is replaced by *L*, while, over at the right, *C* is replaced by *H*. And now the captain of the original U.S.S. *South Dakota* sees *FL* and *JH* in equal distress.

Mon		*AB*	
Tue		*BC*	
Wed	*FB*		*CJ*
Thu	*FL*		*JH*

One of his advisers tells him: The ship on the left is the one that took the maiden voyage on Monday, and the ship on the right, therefore, is not. But another of his advisers tells him: No, it's just the other way around. The ship on the right is the one that took the maiden voyage on Monday, and the ship on the left, therefore, is not. Agreeing on the need for philosophical assistance, the two advisers appeal to a metaphysician who instructs them in the following way: First of all, he says, we must make a technical distinction between what I shall call an intactly persisting temporal object and what I shall call a nonintactly persisting temporal object. A thing is an intactly persisting temporal object if it exists during a period of time and is such that, at any moment of its existence, it has the same parts it had at any other moment of its existence. We may suppose that *AB*, the object that came into being on Monday and passed away on Tuesday, was such an intactly persisting object. So, too, for *BC*, for *FB*, for *CJ*, for *FL*, and for *JH*. Thus a nonintactly persisting temporal object will be a temporal object that is composed of one set of parts at one time and of another set of parts at another time. If we can say of a ship, that it is composed of *A* and B on Monday and composed of *B* and *C* on Tuesday, then a ship is such a nonintactly persisting temporal object."[3]

Appealing now to our diagram, the metaphysician continues: I assume that the situation you disagree about involves the six intact temporal objects you have labeled. It also involves a number of nonintact temporal objects. Thus (i) there is that total object, having the temporal shape of an upside down Y—*that* object is composed of *AB* on Monday, of *BC* on Tuesday, of *FB* and *CD* on Wednesday, and of *FL* and *JH* on Thursday; (ii) there is that object composed of the stem and the left fork of the Y – that object is composed of *AB* on Monday, of *BC* on Tuesday, of *FB* on Wednesday, and of *FL* on Thursday; and (iii) there is that object composed of the stem and of the right fork of the Y – the object that is composed of *AB* on Monday, of *BC* on Tuesday, of *CJ* on Wednesday, and of *JH* on Thursday. The second and third of these temporal objects thus have certain parts in common, and the first one includes both the second and the third among *its* parts.

Given such distinctions as these, our metaphysician now concludes, you can see that there is really nothing for you to dispute about. Just consider the question: Is the ship on the left the one that made the maiden voyage on Monday? If you are asking whether *FL* is identical with *AB*, then the answer is obviously *no*, for *FL* didn't come into being until Thursday and *AB* ceased to exist on Tuesday. On the other hand, if you are asking whether *FL* and *AB* are both parts of our second temporal object, the one composed of the stem and of the left fork of the Y, the answer is clearly *yes*; and *JH* is not a part of that object. And if you are asking whether *JH* and *AB* are both parts of our third temporal object, the one that is composed of the stem and of the right fork of the Y, then the answer, once again, is clearly *yes*; and *FL* is not a part of *that* object. All you need to do then, is to distinguish these various objects and make sure you know *which* ones you are talking about. Then everything will be clear.

I think we might go along with the metaphysician – up to the very last point. Consider the reaction that his sort of instructions might produce: You say that everything will be clear. Things were *far* more clear before you entered the picture. We couldn't agree as to which of these two ships was the one that set sail on Monday. But we were clear, at least, that only two ships were involved. Now, with all your intact and nonintact temporal objects, we have *no* idea how many ships there were. We have learned from Webster that a ship is a structure used for transportation in water. Your intact temporal objects satisfy *that* definition; so they yield at least six ships. What of the nonintact temporal objects? Is the one having the temporal shape of the Y a ship? That would make seven. The stem would give us eight, the two forks would bring it up to ten; the stem plus the left fork makes eleven, and the stem plus the right one makes it *twelve*. Conceivably we might countenance the presence of twelve ships in this situation if by so doing we could solve our problem. But you haven't solved the problem. Consider the poor captain. He wants to go down with his ship and he *still* doesn't know which way to go.

Our metaphysician, I suggest, did not succeed in locating the source of the dispute.

Consider the problem as it pertained to the relation between *FL* (the object that came to be, on the left, on Thursday) and *AB* (the object that had ceased to be by Tuesday). It was agreed that Webster's definition of "x is a ship" would do. It was also agreed that *FL*, *AB*, and the other intact objects satisfied that definition. The question was whether *FL* *constituted the same ship* as did *AB*. And the question whether *FL* constituted the same ship as did *AB* must be distinguished from the closely related question whether *FL was identical with AB*; for, as Locke saw, at least in principle, "*FL* constitutes the same ship as does *AB*" does not imply "*FL* is identical with *AB*."[4]

Railroad trains may provide a more perspicuous example of the distinction between "*x* constitutes the same so-and-so as does *y*" and "*x* is identical with *y*." Suppose we ask: Is this the same train we rode on last year? We are not concerned to know whether the set of objects that makes up today's train is identical with the set of objects that made up the train of a year ago. ("I'm not asking whether we rode on *precisely these same cars* a year ago!") The following three statements tell us three quite different things: (1) This set of cars constitutes a train today and it also constituted a train a year ago; (2) This set of cars constitutes the same train as did that set of cars and that set of cars constituted a train a year ago; (3) This set of cars constitutes the same train that that set of cars constituted a year ago. By going to the dictionary we may find a definition or criterion of "*x* is a train"; but we do not thereby find a definition or criterion of "*x* constitutes the same train as does *y*." A definition of the latter expression would be much more complex and would doubtless say something about roadbeds, schedules, and cities. Possibly, for example, if we can agree that the present aggregate of cars leaves Hoboken at 7:30 P.M. for Chicago via Scranton and the Poconos, we may be willing to concede that this is the same train that we took a year ago, even if all the cars are different. (We may note, in passing, that in this case applicability of "*x* is the same train as *y*" will presuppose applicability of some such expression as "*x* is the same roadbed as was *y*" or "*x* is the same city as was *y*.")

"The same ship" would seem to require a kind of continuity that "the same railroad train" does not. That is to say, if this is to be the same ship that that was, then this ship must be *evolved* in some clear-cut way from that. The requisite sense of "evolves" is illustrated by our diagram. Thus *BC* is continuous with *AB* in that they have a part in common; we may say, therefore, that the latter object *BC* "directly evolved" from the earlier object *AB*. Analogously for the relation of *FB* to *BC*, of *FL* to *FB*, of *CJ* to *BC*, of *JH* to *CJ*, and of *FB* to *AB*. And since *FL* directly evolved from something that evolved from *AB*, we may say simply that *FL* evolved from *AB*.[5]

What more is needed if this to be the same ship that that was? The best we can do, I believe, is to formulate various additional criteria which are such that, if they are satisfied, then this is the same ship that that was. Let us consider only one such criterion—one involving reference to sameness of sailing schedule. Suppose we know, with respect to each object, that it satisfies Webster's definition of a ship: each object is a structure that is used for transportation in water. Suppose we also know that everything that evolved from that and into this was also a structure used for transportation in water (none of these things was ever towed on land and used there as a dwelling-place or as a restaurant). Suppose we know, moreover, that they all followed the same sailing schedule (they were used, say, to ferry passengers between Hoboken and lower Manhattan). And suppose we know, finally, that if at any time one of these objects underwent fission at that time and evolved into more than one structure that was used for transportation in water, then only one of those structures kept to the original schedule. If we know all these things, then, I think, we may say with confidence, that this is the same ship as that—or, more accurately, that this constitutes now the same ship that that constituted then.

Hence one possible criterion (as distinguished from a definition) of "x constitutes now the same ship that y constituted then" would be this: x evolved from y; everything that evolved from y and into x was a structure used for transportation in water and followed the same sailing schedule that y does; and if at any time more than one such structure evolved at that time from y, then only one of them followed the same sailing schedule that y does.

If we should be fortunate enough to find that Wednesday's left hand object followed the same sailing schedule as did those of Monday and Tuesday, and that Wednesday's right hand object took off on a course of its own, then we may conclude that the one on the left, and not the one on the right constitutes the same ship as the one that came to be on Monday.

Reverting to the terminology of our metaphysician, we may say that the situation we have been concerned with involved at least six different intactly persisting objects and at least six different nonintactly persisting objects. Does this mean, then, that the situation involved at least a dozen ships? No, for if we speak in a strict and philosophical sense, we will say that counting ships through a given period of time is not the same as counting structures that are used for transportation in water during that time; it is, rather, to count sets of objects that constitute the same ship during that time. For example, to say that there is *one* ship is to say that there is one set of things all constituting the same ship. To say that there are two ships is to say that there are two sets of things, all the members of the one set constituting the same ship, all the members of the other set constituting the same ship, and no member of the one set constituting the same ship as any member of the other set. And so on, for any number of ships. If, as we are supposing, the *AB*, *BC*, *FB*, and *FL* of our example all follow the same sailing schedule, then they constitute one ship. *CJ*, we said, took off on its own. Hence if *JH* follows the same sailing schedule as did *CJ*, then the situation will involve at most two ships.

We could put the matter paradoxically, therefore, by saying that counting ships is not the same, merely, as counting objects that happen to *be* ships. But if we speak strictly and philosophically, we may avoid any such appearance of paradox. We may say that ships are "logical constructions." The things that they are constructed upon are things that satisfy Webster's definition of the loose and popular sense of "ship"—they are structures used for transportation in water. We will not say, therefore, that *AB*, *BC*, and the other intact structures we discussed *are* ships. We will say, instead, that each of these things constitutes a ship. Given the concept of "x constitutes the same ship as does y," we could define "x constitutes a ship" by saying "x is a member of a set of things all constituting the same ship." The U.S.S. *South Dakota*, therefore, would be a logical construction upon one such set of things. If we continue to speak strictly and philosophically, we will not say of the two different things, *AB* and *FL*, that each of them *is*, on its particular day, the U.S.S. *South Dakota*. We will say instead that each of them *constitutes*, on its particular day, the U.S.S. *South Dakota*. The statements we ordinarily use to describe the ship (e.g., "It weighs more now than it did then") will be reducible to statements about the things that constitute it ("the thing that constitutes it now weighs more than the thing that constituted it then").

We now have an obvious interpretation for the first of theses I have attributed to Bishop Butler—namely, that it is only in a loose and popular sense and not in a strict and philosophical sense that we may speak of the identity of such things as ships through time. He could be construed as telling us, first, that the expression "*x* constitutes at t the same ship that *y* constitutes at *t'* " does *not* imply *x* is identical with *y*"; and analogously for "constituting the same tree," "constituting the same carriage," and so on. Then he could be construed as telling us, second, that if we express the fact that *x* constitutes at one time the same ship that *y* constitutes at another time by saying "*x* is identical with *y*" or "*x* is the same as *y*," then we are speaking only in a loose and popular sense and not in a strict and philosophical sense. And perhaps he could be construed as telling us, finally, that our criteria for *x* constituting the same ship as *y* are pretty much in our own hands, after all, and that once we have determined that a given *x* and *y* do satisfy our criteria for constituting the same ship, or that they do not, then no possible ground for doubt remains.

But there are points of clarification to be made:

(i) In saying that certain uses of language are "loose and popular" rather than "strict and philosophical," we are not suggesting that those uses are *incorrect*. Indeed, they may be said to be *correct*; for it is the loose and popular interpretation rather than the strict and philosophical one that gives the standard of correctness (at any rate, in the loose and popular sense of "correct").

(ii) I have said that it is only in a loose and popular sense that the thing which makes up the U.S.S. *South Dakota* on Thursday may be said to be identical with, or the same as, the thing which made up the U.S.S. *South Dakota* on Monday. But this is *not* to say, of that nonintactly persisting four dimensional temporal object depicted by the stem and the left fork of our upside down Y, that *it* is identical with *itself* only in a loose and popular sense; for that object, like any other, is identical with itself in a strict and philosophical sense. So, too, therefore, for that object made up of the stem and the right fork of the Y, as well as for that object (if our metaphysician was right in assuming that there *is* such as object) made up of the stem plus the right *and* left forks of the Y. Our account of the U.S.S. *South Dakota*, therefore, should not be taken to imply that there are no such four dimensional objects, or that, if there are such, they are not strictly self-identical.

If we could formulate an adequate set of criteria for applying the expression "*x* constitutes the same ship as does *y*" (the one cited above, of course, was only schematic), and if we found that these criteria were satisfied, say, by the original intact object of Monday and the left intact object of Tuesday, then, for the ship that is thus constituted ("*AB* and *FL* both constitute the U.S.S. *South Dakota*"), there would be exactly one nonintact temporal object (namely, the stem and the left fork of the Y). Therefore an alternative to saying that the U.S.S. *South Dakota* is a logical construction upon a set of things all constituting the same ship would be to say that the U.S.S. *South Dakota* is a nonintact temporal object having as its parts at different times the members of a set of things all constituting the same ship. In this case, we could say that the U.S.S. *South Dakota is* the stem and the left fork of the Y.

If we speak in this way, then the point that I have attributed to Bishop Butler will be even more obvious. He would now be telling us that the expression "*x* is a part of the same ship at t that *y* is a part of at *t'* " does not imply "*x* is identical with *y*"; hence if we use the expression "*x* is the same as *y*" or "*x* is identical with *y*" merely to express the fact that "x is a part of the same ship that *y* is a part of," then we are speaking in a loose and popular sense and not in a strict and philosophical sense.[6]

We should remind ourselves, moreover, that merely by referring to *AB* and *FL* as "temporal parts" of one and the same temporal object, we do not thereby answer the question we had put originally as "Does *FL* constitute the same ship as did *AB*?" and that we might now put alternatively as "Is *FL* a temporal part of the same ship as was *AB*?" To simplify the problem even further, consider just two ships, *X* and *Y*, and two days, Monday and Tuesday, through which both ships persist. Let us assume for the moment that there is one set of parts that make up the ship on Monday and another, entirely different set of parts that make up the ship on Tuesday. We may refer to the parts that make up *X* on Mondays as "the Monday parts of *X*" and to the parts that make up *X* on Tuesday as "the Tuesday parts cf *X*." We may now distinguish four pairs of successive aggregates of parts: (1) the Monday parts of *X* and the Tuesday parts of *X*; (2) the Monday parts of *Y* and the Tuesday parts of *Y*; (3) the Monday parts of *X* and the Tuesday parts of *Y*; and (4) the Monday parts of *Y* and the Tuesday parts of *X*. We must therefore choose between two courses. We may say (a) that these four pairs of successive aggregates of parts constitute *four* temporal objects; or we may say (b) that only the first two pairs constitute genuine temporal objects and hence there are only *two* such objects. If we take the first course and say that there are four temporal objects, we will need a criterion for deciding *which* such temporal objects are to be counted as ships; for we would be left with our problem if we said that the third and fourth objects on the list are ships—that the Monday parts of *X* and the Tuesday parts of *Y* make up one ship, and that the Monday parts of *Y* and the Tuesday parts of *X* make up another ship. If we take the second course and say that only the first two pairs of objects on our list are "genuine" temporal objects, then we will need to know what is required for successive temporal parts to be parts of one and the same temporal object.[7]

(iii) Finding an acceptable definition of "*x* is a ship" is a problem for dictionary makers. Finding an acceptable definition of "*x* constitutes the same ship as does *y*" is more likely to be a problem for jurists. It should be noted that we may be in agreement with respect to the proper interpretation of one of those expressions and in disagreement with respect to the proper interpretation of the other; or we may be rigid with respect to the one and latitudinarian with respect to the other.

Assuming we have agreed upon our interpretation of "*x* is a ship," consider the latitude that yet remains with respect to the interpretation of "*x* constitutes the same ship as does *y*." According to the particular criterion of constituting the same ship that was satisfied by our example of the U.S.S. *South Dakota*, today's object and tomorrow's object "constitute the same ship" provided, among other things, that every object that evolves out of today's object and tomorrow's is a ship. And for there to be such evolution, each object, we said, must have some part in common with the object from which it directly evolved. We could say, quoting Hume, that with each step it is "in a manner requisite, that the change of parts be not . . . entire",[8] but it is very possible that we will find it convenient to relax these criteria. Thus it may be useful to be able to say, on occasion, that a certain object of last year constitutes the same ship as does a certain object of this year even though one of the objects, into which last year's object evolved and out of which this year's object evolved, was itself not a ship. Perhaps the ship was partially dismantled and used for a while as a tool shed or as a restaurant; yet, when it was reconverted, we found it convenient, and pleasing to count the result as the same ship that we had before.[9] We may even find it convenient to say on occasion that though a certain object of last year constitutes the same ship as does a certain object of this year, there was no evolution as defined – the change of parts at one stage was entire. Switching for the moment from ships to rivers, consider this situation: We swim in the upper Rio Grande in the early spring; the river dries up in the summer; new waters then flow in and we swim there once again in the fall. Surely we will want our criterion of "*x* constitutes the same river as does *y*" to allow us to say that we swam in the same river twice.

(iv) The expression "*x* constitutes the same ship as does *y*," like "*x* is a ship," allows for borderline cases. We can readily imagine situations in which the only appropriate answer to the question "Is that a ship?" is "Yes and no"–or, better, situations in which "Yes" is no better an answer than "No," and "No" is no better an answer than "Yes."[10] A hydrofoil that is also a hovercraft may serve as an example. We can readily imagine situations in which to the question "Is this the same ship as that?", i.e., "Does this constitute the same ship that that did?", the only answer is "Yes and no."

It may well happen that when we encounter such a borderline case, we must have an answer other than "Yes and no." The captain, as we have seen, may well need a more definite answer, and we may need a definite answer to the question, "Is the combination hydrofoil and hovercraft a ship?", for it may be necessary to decide whether such things are to be subject to the regulations that govern ships or to the regulations that govern aircraft. Similarly, for the question "Does this constitute the same ship that that did?"

When the existence of such a borderline case does thus require us to make a choice between "Yes" and "No" the decision is entirely a pragmatic one, simply a matter of convenience. Which ship is to be called "the Ship of Theseus"—the one that evolved step by step from the original ship, or the one that was assembled from the discarded planks of the original ship? Here we have such a borderline question. The question calls for a convention with respect to the interpretation of "constituting the same ship" (or of "is the same ship as," in its loose and popular sense). We can have it pretty much as we wish, provided we agree. Which ship should the captain go down with? Here, too, we have a borderline question. Perhaps you and I cannot decide, but the courts, or the ships' courts, can decide. If the captain has agreed to go down with the U.S.S. *South Dakota*, and if the court decides that the aluminum ship and not the wooden one is the one that constitutes the U.S.S. *South Dakota*, then down with the aluminum ship he ought to go. Or down with it he ought to go unless the authorities decide subsequently (and in time) to "defeat" the convention they have adopted—for any such convention is defeasible and may be altered or defeated if unexpected circumstances show that it will turn out to be inconvenient. The important thing here is this: The convention of the courts, or of the proper authorities will settle the matter. You and I may object to their decision on the ground that some other decision would have been more convenient. But it would make no sense for us to say: Well, it just might be, you know, that they are mistaken. It just might be that, unknown to them, the wooden ship and not the aluminum one is the U.S.S. *South Dakota*.

(v) There is also a philosophical point to make about our treatment of the problems of the Ship of Theseus and the U.S.S. *South Dakota*.

Speaking of identity or persistence through time, Bishop Butler said: "In a strict and philosophical manner of speech, no man, no being, no mode of being, no anything, can be the same with that with which it hath indeed nothing the same."[11] We may be certain of at least this much: If there is an individual thing x which is such that, through a certain period of time, everything that is part of x at any given moment of that time is also a part of x at any other moment of that time, then what constitutes x at any moment of that time may be said to be identical in the strict and philosophical sense with what constitutes x at any other moment of that time. In such a case, x would satisfy the concept of *intact persistence* that was introduced above. For it was suggested that an individual thing x could be said to *persist intactly* through a given period of time, provided that, at any subperiod of that time, x has the same parts that x has at any other subperiod of that time. In other words, an individual x persists intactly through a given period of time, provided that, for every z, if z is part of x during any subperiod of that time, then z is part of x during every subperiod of that time.[12] Thus we may say that if just one part of our ship is removed or replaced at a certain time, then other parts of the ship, unlike the ship itself, persist intactly through that time.

We formulated above one possible criterion for saying, of different objects at different times, that they constitute one and the same ship. This criterion, it should be noted, presupposes intact persistence, though not intact persistence of the ship; for if the criterion is applicable in the case of a given ship, then, with each step of evolution, some part of the ship remains behind, for the change of parts is "not entire." Hence, with each step, some part persists intactly; some part will be such that it keeps all of *its* parts. But though the evolution of our ship from Monday through Thursday involved intact persistence of some part of the ship at some time during each change that took place, it does not presuppose intact persistence of any part of the ship from Monday through Thursday. We are thus more liberal in our interpretation of "*x* constitutes the same ship as does *y*" than we are, say, in our interpretaion of "*x* constitutes the same bar of metal, or the same piece of wood, or the same hunk of clay as does *y*." For we are not likley to say of *x* that it constitutes the same bar of metal, or the same piece of wood, or the same hunk of clay as does *y*, unless we thing that, throughout the changes from *x* to *y* most of the parts have persisted intactly. But "*x* constitutes the same body of water as does *y*" need not imply that most of the parts have thus persisted intactly. Indeed it need not even imply that the body of water has undergone the type of evolution we described in the case of the ship. Thus, as we have noted, a body of water *x* may constitute in the spring the same river that a body of water *y* constitutes in the fall, even though the river has dried up in the summer and *y*, therefore, has not evolved in the requisite sense from *x*.[13] We might say what St. Thomas said of the river Seine: " . . . the Seine river is not 'this particular river' because of 'this flowing water,' but because of 'this source' and 'this bed,' and hence is always called the same river, although there may be other water flowing down it."[14] Suppose, then, we say that the river of the spring is the same river as the river of the fall in virtue of the fact that the river of the spring flows through *the same river bed* as does the river of the fall. What, then, would be our criterion for saying that something *x* in the spring is the same river bed as something *y* in the fall? It might be the fact that the river bed in the fall has evolved in the manner I have attempted to describe from the river bed in the spring. Or it might be that the material that constitutes the river bed in the spring is found *the same river banks* as is the material that constitutes the river bed in the fall. We might then say that *x* in the spring constitutes the same river bank as does *y* in the fall if, once again, *y* has evolved from *x* in the manner I have described.[15]

In other words, persistence, in the loose and popular sense, through time would seem to presuppose such evolution; and such evolution, in turn, presupposes persistence, in the strict and philosophical sense, through time. For it presupposes what I have called intact persistence. It is not implausible to say, therefore, that if there is anything that persists, in the loose and popular sense, through any given period of time, then there is something (perhaps not the same thing) that persists intactly through some subperiod of that time.

What now of Bishop Butler's second thesis—the thesis according to which, when we say of a *person* existing at one time that he is identical with a person existing at another time, we are likely to be using "identical" in a strict and philosophical sense and not merely in a loose and popular sense?

I have suggested a possible interpretation of the expression "loose and popular sense of the *same*." Putting the point schematically, we may say that "*x* is the same *F* as *y*" is used in a loose and popular sense if it is used in such a way that it does not imply "*x* is identical with *y*." (The expression "*x* constitutes the same *F* as does *y*" would thus be less misleading for such a use.) I have also suggested that when "*x* is the same *F* as *y*" is used in this loose and popular sense, then it is possible to imagine conditions under which a question of the form "Is *x* the same *F* as *y*?" has no definite answer—conditions under which we may say both "Yes" and "No," for "Yes" will be as good an answer as "No," and "No" will be as good an answer as "Yes."

Such an interpretation of the expression "loose and popular sense of *same*" suggests at once a possible interpretation of the expression "strict and philosophical sense of *same*." For example, we are using the expression "*x* is the same person as *y*" in a strict and philosophical sense if we are using it in such a way that it implies "*x* is identical with *y*." In this case "*x* is the same person as *y*" will be logically equivalent to "*x* is a person and *x* is identical with *y*." I wish to suggest that "*x* is the same person as *y*," where the expression in the place of "*x*" is taken to designate a certain person at existing at one time and where the expression in the place of "*y*" is taken to designate a certain person existing at a different time, does have this strict and philosophical use.

When we use "the same person" in this strict way, then, although cases may well arise in which we have no way of *deciding* whether the person *x* is the same person as the person *y*, nevertheless the question "Is *x* the same person as *y*?" will *have* an answer and that answer will be either "Yes" or "No." If we know that *x* is a person and if we also know that *y* is a person, then it is not possible to imagine circumstances under which the question "Is *x* the same person as *y*?" is a border-line question—a question admitting only of a "Yes and no" answer.

The latter point may be illustrated in the following way. If *x* knows, with respect to some set of properties, that there is or will be a person *y* who will have these properties at some future date, then *x* may ask himself "*Will I be he?*" and to that question the answer must be "Yes" or "No." For either *x* is identical with *y* or *x* is not identical with *y*.

If it is clear that if *x* is a person and *y* is a person, then we cannot answer the question "Is *x* the same person as *y*?" merely by deciding what would be practically convenient. To be sure, if we lack sufficient evidence for making a decision, it may yet be necessary for the courts to *rule* that *x* is the same person as *y*, or that he is not. Perhaps the ruling will have to be based upon practical considerations and conceivably such considerations may lead the court later to "defeat" their ruling. But if Bishop Butler, as I have interpreted him, is right, then one may always ask of any such ruling "But is it *correct*, or *true*?" For a ruling to the effect that *x* is the same person as *y* will be correct, or true, only if *x* is identical with *y*.

Here, then, we have one possible interpretation of the thesis that, in one of its important uses, the expression "*x* is the same person as *y*" must be interpreted in a strict and philosophical sense. It seems clear to me that "*x* is the same person as *y*" does have this use. Whenever a person *x* asks himself, with respect to some person *y*, "Will I be he?" or "Was that person I?" then the answer to his question, if put in the form "*x* is the same person as *y*," or "*x* is not the same person as *y*," must be taken in the strict and philosophical sense.

We should remind ourselves, however, that the expression "x is the same person as y" also has a use which is not this strict and philosophical one. Thus there are circumstances in which one might say: "Mr. Jones is not at all the same person he used to be. You will be disappointed. He is not the person that you remember." We would not say this sort of thing if Mr. Jones had changed only slightly. We would say it only if he had undergone changes that were quite basic and thoroughgoing—the kind of changes that might be produced by psychoanalysis or by a lobotomy, or by a series of personal tragedies. But just *how* basic and thoroughgoing must these changes be if we are to say of Mr. Jones that he is a different person? The proper answer would seem to be: As basic and thoroughgoing as you would like. It's just a matter of convention. It all depends upon how widely it is convenient for you to construe the expression "He's the same person he used to be." Insofar as the rules of language are in your own hands, you may have it any way you would like. (Compare "Jones is not himself today" or "Jones was not himself when he said that.")

This, however, is only a "loose and popular" sense of identity. When we say, in this sense, "Jones is no longer the person he used to be," we do not mean that there is, or was, a certain entity such that Jones was formerly identical with that entity and is no longer so. We do not mean to imply that there are (or have been) certain entities, x and y, such that at one time x is, or was, identical with y, and at another time x is not identical with y. For this, I believe, is incoherent, but "Jones is no longer the person he used to be" is not.

Nor do we mean, when we say "Jones is no longer the person he used to be," that there *was* a certain entity, the old Jones, which no longer exists, and that there is a certain *different* entity, the new Jones, which somehow has taken his place. We are not describing the kind of change that takes place when one President succeeds another. In the latter case, there is a clear answer to the question "What happened to the old one?" The answer might be "He was shot" or "He retired to Gettysburg." But when we decide to call Jones a new person, we are not confronted with such questions as: What happened, then, to the old Jones? Did he die, or was he annihilated, or disassembled, or did he retire to some other place?

The old Jones did not die; he was not annihilated or disassembled; and he did not retire to any other place. He *became* the new Jones. To say that he "became" the new Jones is *not* to say that he "became identical" with something he hadn't been identical with before; for it is only when a thing comes into being that it may be said to become identical with something it hadn't been identical with before. To say that our man "became the new Jones" is to say only that he, Jones, *altered* in a significant way, taking on certain interesting properties he had not had before. (Hence we should contrast the "became" of "Jones then became a married man," said when Jones ceased to be a bachelor, with that of "The President then became a Democrat," said when President Eisenhower retired.) When we say of a thing that *it* has properties that *it* did not have before, we are saying that there is an x such that x formerly had such-and-such properties and x presently has such-and-such properties. But to say that there is an x, at least one x, such that x was now this and x is now that, would seem to presuppose the identity of x through time, in *some* sense of the term "identity." Is the sense of identity that is presupposed merely that in which we can say of any temporal object, intact or nonintact, that it is identical with itself? Or are we also presupposing that, in the strict and philosophical sense, whatever goes to make up that person now is identical with whatever went to make him up at the earlier time?[16]

One may well ask: But *need* we presuppose this? Need we presuppose the persistence of a single subject of change when, as we say, the man becomes "a new person?" To appreciate the situation, it may be necessary to imagine that the person in question is oneself. Suppose, then, that you were such a person—that you had undergone basic and thoroughgoing changes and that your friends and acquaintances were in agreement that you are no longer the same person that you were. What, then, if you *remember* all the relevant facts—that *you* had formerly been a person of such-and-such a sort, that you had undergone certain shattering experiences, and that these then led to a transformation in your personality, with the result that you are not the person that *you* formerly were?

Let us imagine, however, that your friends and acquaintances say to you: "But you are such a *very* different person now that henceforth we are going to treat you like one. We will call you "Smith" instead of "Jones." We will make certain that you are free from all the obligations that Jones incurred. And if you feel guilty about some of the wicked things that Jones did, you need no longer have such feelings, for we can get the highest courts to lay it down that you are two quite different people. Something, surely, is wrong here.

Some people, I have found, see at once that something is wrong and others do not. For those who do not, let me propose that we look in a different direction. What would we think of such talk if we were to hear it *before* rather than after the transformation of our personality?

It will be instructive to elaborate upon an example that C. S. Peirce suggests.[17] Let us assume that you are about to undergo an operation and that you still have a decision to make. The utilities involved are, first, financial—you wish to avoid any needless expense—and, secondly, the avoidance of pain, the avoidance, however, just of *your* pain, for pain that is other than yours, let us assume, is of no concern whatever to you. The doctor proposes two operating procedures—one a very expensive procedure in which you will be subjected to total anaesthesia and no pain will be felt at all, and the other of a rather different sort. The second operation will be very inexpensive indeed; there will be no anaesthesia at all and therefore there will be excruciating pain. But the doctor will give you two drugs: first, a drug just before the operation which will induce complete amnesia, so that while you are on the table you will have no memory whatever of your present life; and secondly, just after the agony is over, a drug that will make you completely forget everything that happened on the table. The question is: Given the utilities involved, namely the avoidance of needless expense and the avoidance of pain that *you* will feel, other pains not mattering, is it reasonable for you to opt for the less expensive operation?

My own belief is that it would *not* be reasonable, even if you could be completely certain that both amnesia injections would be successful. I think that *you* are the one who would undergo that pain, even though you, Jones, would not know at the time that it is Jones who is undergoing it, and even though you would never remember it. Consider after all, the hypothesis that it would *not* be you. What would be your status, in such a case, during the time of the operation? Would you be waiting in the wings somewhere for the second injection, and if so, where? Or would you have passed away? That is to say, would you have *ceased* to *be*, but with the guarantee that you—you, yourself—would come into being once again when the *agony* was over?[18] And what about the person who *would* be feeling the pain? Who would he be?

I can appreciate that these things might not seem obvious to you as you ponder your decision. You may wonder: "I would certainly like to save that money. Will it really be *I* who feels that pain? How can it be if I won't know that it's I?" Perhaps you would have some ground for hesitation. But there is one point, I think, that ought to be obvious.

Suppose that others come to you—friends, relatives, judges, clergymen—and they offer the following advice and assurance. "Have no fear," they will say, "Take the cheaper operation and we will take care of everything. We will lay it down that the man on the table is not you, Jones, but is Smith. We will not allow this occasion to be mentioned in your biography. And during the time that you lie there on the table—excuse us (they will interject), we mean to say, during the time that *Smith* lies there on the table—we will say, 'poor Smith' and we will not say, even in our hearts, 'poor Jones.' " What *ought* to be obvious to you, it seems to me, is that the laying down of this convention should have no effect at all upon your decision. For you may still ask, "But won't that person be I?" and, it seems to me, the question has an answer.

Suppose you know that your body, like that of an amoeba, would one day undergo fission and that you would go off, so to speak, in two different directions. Suppose you also know, somehow, that the one who went off to the left would experience the most wretched of lives and that the one who went off to the right would experience a life of great happiness and value. If I am right in saying that one's question "Will that person be I?" or "Will I be he?" always has a definite answer, then, I think, we may draw these conclusions. There is no possibility whatever that *you* would be *both* the person on the right and the person on the left. Moreover, there *is* a possibility that you would be one or the other of those two persons. And, finally, *you* could be one of those persons and yet have no memory at all of your present existence.[19] It follows that it would be reasonable of you, if you are concerned with *your* future pleasures and pains, to hope that you will be the one on the right and not the one on the left—also that it would be reasonable of you, given such self-concern, to have this hope even if you know that the one on the right would have no memory of your present existence. Indeed it would be reasonable of you to have it even if you know that the one on the *left* thought he remembered the facts of your present existence.[20] And it seems to me to be absolutely certain that no fears that you might have, about being the half on the left, could reasonably be allayed by the adoption of a convention, or by the formulation of a criterion, even if our procedure were endorsed by the highest authorities.

Notes

I am indebted to John Wisdom, Sydney Shoemaker, and Fred Feldman for criticisms of earlier versions of this paper. Certain paragraphs have been adapted from my "The Loose and Popular and the Strict and Philosophical Senses of Identity," in Norman S. Care and Robert H. Grimm (eds.), *Perception and Personal Identity*, by permission of Case Western Reserve University Press, Cleveland.

1. "Of Personal Identity," Dissertation I, in *The Whole Works of Joseph Butler*, LL. D. (London: Thomas Tegg, 1839), pp. 263–270. The dissertation is reprinted in Antony Flew, (ed.), *Body, Mind and Death* (New York: Macmillan, 1964), pp. 166–72.

2. Thomas Hobbes, *Concerning Body*, Chap. II ("Of Identity and Difference"), Sec. 7.

3. But a nonintactly persisting temporal object should be distinguished from what I shall call an "Edwardian" temporal object (after Jonathan Edwards). An Edwardian temporal object would be a temporal object which is such that, for each moment during which it exists, there is a set of parts which are what make up that object at that moment and which exist only at that moment. Hence if x is an Edwardian temporal object, then for any two times, t and t' at which x exists, there is one set of objects which make up x at t, and another set of objects which make up x at t', and no member of the first set has any part in common with any member of the second set. If, as some philosophers have supposed, all temporal objects are Edwardian, then no object which persists through a period of time could be said to persist intactly, as this term was defined by our metaphysician above; for no object would be such that it has the same parts at any moment of its existence that it has at any other moment of its existence. This extreme Edwardian view was defended by J. H. Woodger in *The Axiomatic Method in Biology* (Cambridge: The University Press, 1937) and by Rudolf Carnap in *Introduction to Symbolic Logic* (New York: Dover Publications, 1958), see pp. 213–16. Jonathan Edwards took this extreme view to be implied by "God's upholding created substance, or causing its existence in each successive moment." For, he reasoned, "if the existence of created *substance*, in each successive moment, be wholly the effect of God's immediate power, in *that* moment, without any dependence on prior existence, as much as the first creation out of *nothing*, then what exists at this moment, by this power, is a *new effect*, and simply and absolutely considered, not the same with any past existence. . . . " From this he was able to deduce that it is as reasonable and just to impute Adam's original sin to me now as it is to impute any sin which I may seem to remember having committed myself. (See the *Doctrine of Original Sin Defended*, Part 4, Chap. 2.) But this extreme view, when considered separately from the doctrine of divine re-creation, has at least the disadvantage of multiplying entities beyond necessity. (Compare: "John is kind toward Mary and unkind toward Alice; therefore there is something, namely John-toward-Mary, that is kind, and there is something, namely John-toward-Alice, that is unkind, and these two different things go to make up John.") It should not be attributed to our metaphysician above.

4. See Locke's *Essay*, Book II, Chap. 27, Sec. 5, 6, and 8. The point made above does not, of course, imply the more extreme thesis, according to which a statement of the form, "x is identical with y," is always elliptical for one of the form, "x is the same F as y."

5. These concepts might be defined as follows: x *evolves directly* from y, provided: either x is identical with y, or there is no time at which x and y both exist but there is a z such that z is part of y at one time and z is part of x at a later time. (Possibly we should add that, during any subperiod between the earlier and the later time, z has the same parts that it has during any other such subperiod.) And, more generally, x *evolves* from y, provided: x is a member of every class C such that (i) y is a member of C and (ii) whatever directly evolves from anything that is a member of C is also a member of C. (If the definition of "evolves directly" were intended to explicate the ordinary use of this expression, it would doubtless be too broad; but it is not so intended.)

6. We should take care not to misinterpret Butler at this point. In saying that "this is the same ship as that" is to be understood only in a loose and popular sense and not in a strict and philosophical sense, he is taking the "this" and the "that" to refer to the particular objects that, on their respective days, constitute (or serve as the parts of) the ship in question on those days; he is not using "this" or "that" to refer to the set of things that constitute the ship, or to the nonintact temporal object of which those things may be construed as parts. This is clear, I think, from the following passage: "For when a man swears to the same tree as having stood fifty years in the same place, he means only the same as to all the purposes of property and uses of common life, and not that the tree has been all that time the same in the strict and philosophical sense of the word. For he does not know whether any one particle of the present tree be the same with any one particle of the tree which stood in the same place fifty years ago."

7. Our example involves just four pairs of objects. Consider the number of ostensible temporal objects, or ostensible ships, we would have to choose among, if we added just one more ship and one more day to our example. Or the objects that would be involved if all temporal objects were "Edwardian," as this term was defined in footnote 3 above (The account that I have given of the history of the U.S.S. *South Dakota* presupposes that there are some intactly persisting temporal objects, and therefore it is inconsistent with the view that all temporal objects are Edwardian.)

8. *Treatise*, Book I, Part 4, Sec. vi.

9. An Aristotelian who took ships seriously might say that in such a case two "substantial changes" had occurred.

10. I owe this way of putting the matter to Professor John Wisdom who criticized an earlier version of this paper at Lewis and Clark College in October 1967.

11. "Of Personal Identity," in Flew, *Body, Mind and Death*, p. 265.

12. What if the parts of a thing are "simply re-arranged"—say, from ABC to CAB? If we take the term "part" in its ordinary sense, as I propose that we do, then we must say that the thing will not have persisted intactly, for it will have lost some parts. If the thing changes from ABC to CAB, then it will lose BC, as well as that part that consists of the right half of B and the left half of C.

If we could say, however, that compound things are composed of "ultimate particles" which are not themselves composed of parts, then we could formulate a definition of "intact persistence" which would allow us to say that a thing may persist intactly through rearrangement of its parts. For we could say that a thing persists intactly through a given period of time if, at any subperiod of that time, it has the same "ultimate particles" that it has at any other period of that time. Thus Locke said that, so long as any group of "atoms" (ultimate particles) "exist united together, the mass, consisting of the same atoms, must be the same mass, or the same body, let the parts be ever so differently jumbled. But if one of these atoms be taken away, or one now one added, it is no longer the same mass or the same body." (*Essay*, Book II, Chap. 27, Sec. 4. This use of "same," I am sure he would have agreed, is strict and philosophical and not loose and popular.)

13. For further possibilities, see Helen M. Cartwright, "Heraclitus and the Bath Water," *Philosophical Review*, 74 (1965): 466–84.

14. *De Spiritualibus Creaturis*, Article IX, ad. 16; translated as "On Spiritual Creatures," by M. C. Fitzpatrick and J. J. Wollmuth (Milwaukee, Marquette University Press, 1949). See p. 109 of the translation.

15. One might be tempted to define sameness of river bank or of river bed, say, in terms of *sameness of place*. If sameness of place is not then defined in terms of a relation to things that are said to exist in space, such a definition would seem to presuppose intact persistence of substantival space through time. (It may be noted, incidentally, that our account of "evolving" allows us to say that a thing at a later date evolves from a thing at an earlier date even though there has been no change of parts.)

16. It should be noted that, although the loose and popular use in question is one in which "*x* is *not* the same person as *y*" is consistent with "*x is* identical with *y*," it is not a use in which "*x is* the same person as *y*" is consistent with "*x* is *not* identical with *y*." It is difficult to think of any actual examples of the latter type of use. Perhaps those who takes roles more seriously than they do persons

might say such things as "Elizabeth is the same monarch as Victoria was" while aware of the falsehood of the corresponding identity statement. But such uses, fortunately, are not ordinary.

17. " 'If the power to remember dies with the material body, has the question of any single person's future life after death any particular interest for him?' As you put the question, it is not whether the matter ought rationally to have an interest but whether as a fact it has; and perhaps this is the proper question, trusting as it seems to do rather to instinct than to reason. Now if we had a drug which would abolish memory for a while, and you were going to be cut for the stone, suppose the surgeon were to say, 'You will suffer damnably, but I will administer this drug so that you will during that suffering lose all memory of your previous life. Now you have, of course, no particular interest in your suffering as long as you will not remember your present and past life, you know, have you?' " *Collected Papers*, vol. 5 (Cambridge, Mass.: Harvard University Press, 1935), p. 355.

18. See Locke's *Essay*, Book II, Chap. xxvii, Sec. i: "One thing cannot have two beginnings of existence." Compare Thomas Reid, *Essays on the Intellectual Powers of Man*, Essay III, Chap. 4.

19. In this case, there might well be no *criterion* by means of which you or anyone else could decide which of the two halves was in fact yourself. I would agree with Shoemaker's contention that "our ability to know first-person psychological statements to be true, or the fact that we make them (for the most part) only when they are true, cannot possibly be explained on the supposition that we make them on the basis of criteria": Sydney Shoemaker, *Self-Knowledge and Self-Identity* (Ithaca, N.Y.: Cornell University Press, 1963), p. 214. One consequence of this fact, I suggest, is the following: it makes sense to suppose in connection with the above example that you are in fact the half that goes off to the left and not the one that goes off to the right even though there is no criterion at all by means of which anyone could decide the matter. I would disagree, incidentally, with what Shoemaker says (pp. 236–38) about the relationship between criteria and necessary truths—at least, if "necessary" is taken to mean the same as "logically necessary." My own views on this question may be suggested by Chap. 4 ("The Problem of the Criterion") in my *Theory of Knowledge* (Englewood Cliffs, N.J.: Prentice-Hall, 1966).

20. I would endorse, therefore, the following observation that Bayle makes in his article on Lucretius (see Note Q of "Lucretius," in Pierre Bayle, *A General Dictionary, Historical and Critical*): "The same atoms which compose water, are in ice, in vapours, in clouds, in hail and snow; those which compose wheat, are in the meal, in the bread, the blood, the flesh, the bones etc. Were they unhappy under the figure or form of water, and under that of ice, it would be the same numerical substance that would be unhappy in those two conditions; and consequently all the calamities which are to be dreaded, under the form of meal, concern the atoms which form corn; and nothing ought to concern itself so much about the state or lot of the meal, as the atoms which form the wheat, though they are not to suffer these calamities, under the form of wheat." Bayle concludes that "there are but two methods a man can employ to calm, in a rational manner, the fears of another life. One is, to promise himself the felicities of Paradise; the other, to be firmly persuaded that he shall be deprived of sensations of every kind."

5

Possibility without Haecceity

The Problem of the Merely Possible

The "problem of the merely possible" is that of describing the merely possible without supposing that there is a realm of *possibilia* falling between being and nonbeing and without violating the principles of contradiction and excluded middle. To solve the problem, one may make use of one or the other of the following two locutions:

(A) x is possible such that he is an *F*;

(B) There is a (possible) world in which *x* is an *F*.

Some philosophers would attempt to explicate (A) in terms of (B). Suppose I am not a physician but could have been one. Then these philosophers would say that there are possible worlds other than the actual one and that I *am* a physician in those worlds. If this explication is to work, then a possible world must be an entity that is capable of *containing* me. But what is the relevant sense of "in" or "contain?" We may give a meaning to this use of such expressions if we can say that I have an individual essence or haecceity—a set of properties that are "essential to me and repugnant to everything else." We could say, more generally, that an individual thing *x* exists *in* a possible world *w* provided that the haecceity of *x* is exemplified in *W*.

There is, then, an enormous amount of metaphysics involved in explicating (A) in terms of (B). And, so, let us try to do things the other way around. I will suggest that if (B) is to make any sense, it must be explicated in terms of (A).

How are we to choose between these two approaches to the question? We can ask which one presupposes the simpler ontology. The view that I will set forth does not presuppose that *in addition* to individuals, properties and relations, and states of affairs, there are such things as possible worlds *in* which particular in-

42

dividuals such as you and I may be said to exist. Therefore, we do not need to cope with the problem of "transworld identity," and our view does not require us to presuppose that individual things have individual essences or haecceities.

I will, then, make use of the undefined *de re* locution "*x* is possible such that it is *F*" and the other modal locutions that may be defined in terms of it. And I will make use of the concepts of properties, relations, and states of affairs.

Worlds Defined

I will begin with a conception of "possible world" — but I will say just "world" — which is essentially that of Leibniz and other philosophers in the Western tradition. It is unlike that presupposed by most contemporary philosophers.

> D1 *W* is a world = *Df W* is a state of affairs; for every state of affairs *p*, either *W* logically implies *p* or *W* logically implies the negation of *p*; and there is no state of affairs *q* such that *W* logically implies both *q* and the negation of *q*.

A world, then, is a self-consistent, maximal state of affairs. That it is maximal is guaranteed by the first clause of our definition; that it is self-consistent is guaranteed by the second.[1] A world is thus a *conjunctive* state of affairs.

I have defined "a *world*," not "a *possible* world." I have avoided "possible world," since the expression "There are possible worlds" may suggest that there *are* certain things — worlds — that neither exist nor fail to exist and that fall between being and nonbeing. I believe that the concept philosophers have traditionally had in mind when speaking of "possible worlds" can be explicated by reference to those states of affairs that are here called "worlds."[2] If this is so, and if, as I believe, states of affairs are abstract objects existing whether or not they obtain, then *all* so-called "possible worlds" exist. Hence, I use "world," and not "possible world."

"But you can't mean to say that all possible worlds are *actual* worlds. There is — and can be — only *one* actual world!" The word "actual" here is ambiguous. If "*x* is actual" is taken to mean the same as "*x exists*," then all possible worlds are actual. But when it is said that only *one* world is actual, then "*x* is actual" is taken to mean the same as "*x obtains.*" There is — and can be — only one world that obtains.

It is well to avoid the temptation to speak of "the real world" or "the actual world." Let us, rather, speak of "the *world that obtains*" or "the *prevailing world.*"

What is the Essence of a Thing?

Traditionally, the essence of a thing was said to be a property that is essential to the thing and necessarily repugnant to everything else. The following definition may therefore suggest itself:

E is the essence of $x = Df\, x$ is necessarily such that it has E; and for all y, if y is other than x, then y is necessarily such that it does not have E.

But the second clause is not strong enough. Suppose (i) I am necessarily such that I am a person, (ii) all nonpersons are necessarily such that they are nonpersons, and (iii) I am the only person there is. Given the proposed definition, it would follow from these assumptions that the property of being a person is my essence. But it would not follow that being a person is necessarily repugnant to everything else.

How, then, are we to strengthen the second clause in the definition? Shall we say: "It is not possible for there to be a y such that y is other than x and y has E"? This would have to be reducible to our *de re* locution, "x is possibly such that it is F." What we should say is rather this: "x is not possibly such that there is a y such that y is other than x and y has E." Our definition will be:

D2 E is the essence of $x = Df\, x$ is necessarily such that it has E; for every property P, if x is necessarily such it has P, then E implies P; and x is not possibly such that there is a y other than x such that y has E.

Given our definition of essence, we may now say what an *abstract object* is: it is a thing having an essence that is such that *everything* is necessarily such that there is something having that essence. The essence of the property *blue* is the property of being a thing that is necessarily such that it is exemplified in all and only those things that are blue. And if, as I believe, the property blue is an abstract object, then everything is necessarily such that there is something that is necessarily such that it is exemplified in all and only those things that are blue. We will say, then:

D3 x is an abstract object $= Df$ There is an E that is such that (a) E is the essence of x and (b) everything is necessarily such that there is something that has E.

I will assume that properties, relations, and states of affairs are all abstract objects. I will also assume that individual things—such entities as you and me—are not abstract objects. It will follow (1) that everything is necessarily such that abstract objects exist and (2) that no abstract object is necessarily such that any individual thing exists.

Existing in a World

The conception of a *world* that has just been set forth is to be contrasted with that held by many contemporary philosophers. Worlds, according to them, are things *in* which—in some unanalyzed sense of "in"—individuals such as you and me are to be found. But if a world is a state of affairs, and if states of affairs are abstract or eternal objects, what could it mean to say of an *individual thing* that it exists "in a world"? How could you or I exist "in" an abstract object?

We may *give* a meaning to this use of "in." We could say, for example, that if a world implies the property of being a dog, then at least one dog exists "in" that world. (A state of affairs may be said to imply a given property provided only that the state of affairs is necessarily such that, if it obtains, then something has that property.) Hence, we might say similarly that if a thing *x* has an essence, and if a given world implies that essence, then *x* exists "in" that world. And we can also say that everything exists "in" the world that obtains. Let us say, then:

D4 *x* exists in *W* = *Df W* is a world; and either (a) *x* has an essence *E* such that *W* implies *E* or (b) *W* obtains and *x* exists.

Possibilities without Haecceities

The word "haecceity" has traditionally been used to mean the same as "individual essence," or "essence of an individual thing." Let us use the word in this way:

D5 *H* is the haecceity of *x* = *Df x* is an individual thing: and *H* is the essence of *x*.

Is there any reason for supposing that there *are* haecceities—that individual things *have* essences?

Many believe that the doctrine that there are individual essences follows from the assumption that individual things have unrealized possibilities. The reasoning may be illustrated this way: "(1) I am not a physician. Therefore, (2) there is a world *W* that is other than the world that obtains and that is such that I am a physician *in W*. But (3) if I exist in a world that does not obtain, then I have an essence. (This follows from D4—our definition of what it is to exist *in* a world.) Therefore, (4) I have an essence."

But (2) does not follow from (1). Let us consider how we might describe my unrealized possibilities without assuming that I have an individual essence.

Even if I do not have an individual essence, *some* of my properties are essential to me—i.e., some of my properties are such that I have them necessarily. Suppose that *being a person* is such a property. Now there are some worlds that do not imply the property of being a person ("Some possible worlds don't contain any persons"). If I am necessarily a person, then I am necessarily such that none of those impersonal worlds obtain. We may say that I *exclude* such worlds. (Or we could put it the other way around and say that I am such that I am excluded by certain worlds.) For we may say that a thing *x excludes* a world *W*, provided only that *x* is necessarily such that *W* does not obtain.

It is important to note that from the fact that I am *not* excluded by a certain world *W*, it does not follow that I *exist in* that world *W*. But if I am not excluded by *W*, then I am *eligible* for *W*; that is, I am possibly such that *W* obtains.

If I were to have an essence *E* such that there is a certain world *W* that implies *E* (i.e., a certain world *W* that is necessarily such that if it obtains then something exemplifies *E*), then we could say that *W* is necessarily such that I exist. But if

I have no individual essence, then we cannot say of *any* world that it is necessarily such that I exist. And we cannot even say this of "the actual world"—i.e., the world that obtains. The latter point may be put somewhat loosely by saying that this world could have obtained without me. If the world had obtained without me, then someone else would have played the role that I happen to play in this world. Indeed, if neither you nor I have individual essences, then the prevailing world could have obtained with you playing my role and me playing yours. One might say, paradoxically, that you and I would have been very different but the world would have been the same; this gives us a use for the label "existentialism."[3]

We cannot say, therefore, that "*x* exists in *W*"means the same as "If *W* were to obtain, then *x* would exist." For I exist in this world, but this world could have obtained without me.

An Objection Considered

Consider now an objection to what we have been saying: "(1) Your theory implies this: that world W^1 is identical with a world W^2 if and only if W^1 implies the same states of affairs that W^2 implies. But (2) it is possible (a) that there is a world W^1 implying exactly the same properties as are implied by a world W^2 and yet (b) W^1 may be such that a certain person—say, Jones—is in it, and W^2 may be such that Jones is not in it. Therefore (3) your theory is false."

We are now in a position to see that even if the existentialistic intuition is true, the second premise of the argument is false. The point is not that there are two worlds, W^1 and W^2, such that Jones is "in" one of them and not "in" the other. It is, rather, that there is a world W^1 ($= W^2$) that is such that Jones is eligible for W^1 but does not have an essence that W^1 implies. One might also put this by saying: W^1 is possibly such that it obtains and Jones does not exist. Jones is "in" W^1, but W^1 could have obtained without him.

To say that you and I "could have changed places" in W^1 is to say this: there is a certain set A of properties such that I have the members of A; there is another set B of properties such that you have the members of B; I am possibly such that I have the members of B and W^1 obtains; and you are possibly such that you have the members of A and W^1 obtains.

We should distinguish the following locutions:

(p) It is possible there are no persons;
(q) I am such that possibly there are no persons;
(r) I am possibly such that there are no persons;
(s) I am possibly such that I exist and there are no persons.

There is an ambiguity in (r), for it may be taken to say the same thing as (q), or it may be taken to say the same thing as (s). But although (s) implies (q), it is not the case the (q) implies (s). For if I am essentially a person, then although (p) and (q) will be true, (s) will be false.

Suppose a thing has a certain property necessarily. What does this imply with respect to those characteristics that the prevailing world has necessarily? Next to nothing, I would say. For example, Socrates may be necessarily such that he is a person. It does not follow from this either (a) that Socrates is necessarily such that he is a *person in this world*, or (b) that this world is necessarily such that Socrates exists and is a person.

The fact that I exist only in the prevailing world—if it is a fact—does not restrict my possibilities. The unrealized possibilities of a given individual are not to be explicated in terms of the different worlds in which that individual might be said to exist. We may speak of such possibilities, using the undefined *de re* modal locution with which we began: "*x* is possibly such that it is *F*." And so we may say of a person who is not a physician that "he could have been a physician." This does not tell us that he is a physician "in some possible world." It tells us no more nor less than that he is possibly such that he is a physician—that none of his essential properties are incompatible with being a physician. "He is possibly such that he is a physician" does *not* tell us that he has a nature that is compatible with being a physician. For what would this "nature" be if the person does not have an individual essence? "He is possibly such that he is a physician" tells us, rather, that he does *not* have an essence that is *incompatible* with his being a physician.

"If he is possibly such that he is a physician, and if he's not a physician in the prevailing world, then isn't it the case that, if he *were* a physician, he would be a physician *in another world?*" This may be correct. But from this fact it does not follow that he *is* a physician in any other world. For unless he has an individual essence, any other world could obtain without him.

An Argument for the Doctrine of Haecceities

Alvin Plantinga writes: "Is there any reason to suppose that 'being identical with Socrates' names a property? Well, is there any reason to suppose that it does not? . . . Surely it is true of Socrates that he is Socrates and that he is identical with Socrates. If these are true of him, then *being Socrates* and *being identical with Socrates* characterize him; they are among his properties or attributes".[4] One could argue similarly, as I did in the book *Person and Object*, that the expression "being me" has the property *being me* as its sense and that the property of *being me* is essential to me and repugnant to everything else. Then one could conclude that *being me* is my haecceity.

But why assume that terms such as "Socrates" and "I" *have* senses? One can describe their use adequately without such an assumption. The function of proper names in a language may be described without presupposing that they have senses. The same applies to pronouns and demonstratives. We may say that the primary use of the locution "I am *F*" in English is that of conveying that one has attributed to oneself the property of being *F*. The primary use of "*That* is *F*" is that of conveying that the thing one is calling attention to has the property of being *F*.[5]

Of course, it is true that Socrates is necessarily identical with Socrates and that I am necessarily me. But I see no reason for supposing that these statements commit us to anything other than Socrates, me, and the property of being self-identical.[6] What if one were to say: "That thing is necessarily identical with that thing; therefore, there is the property of *being identical with that thing* that constitutes the sense of 'that thing' "? How do I distinguish this property from the one I may refer to later when, pointing to a different object, I say: "And that thing is necessarily identical with that thing"? Surely I don't contemplate two essences, one for the first occurrence of "that thing" and another for the second.

It has even been suggested that those haecceities that constitute the senses of "Socrates," "that thing," and "me," respectively, are ontologically dependent upon Socrates, that thing, and me. To say that one thing is "ontologically dependent" upon another is, I suppose, to say that the first thing is necessarily such that the second exists. But if what I have suggested is correct, haecceities are abstract objects, and no abstract object is dependent for its being upon any particular thing.

I see no reason, then, to assume that the fact of unrealized possibilities presupposes that individual things have essences or haecceities.

Notes

1. If we wanted to say that there are also "impossible worlds," we should remove the final clause from the definiens. But no useful purpose is served by speaking in this way.

2. Compare Leibniz, *Theodicy* (London: Routledge and Kegan Paul, 1952), part III, sec. 414: "These worlds are all here, that is, in ideas [*Ces Mondes sont tous ici, c'est-à-dire en idées*]. I will show you some, wherein shall be found, not absolutely the same Sextus as you have seen (that is not possible, he carries with him always that which he shall be) but several Sextuses resembling him." Compare C. I. Lewis, *An Analysis of Knowledge and Valuation* (La Salle, Ill.: Open Court, 1946), Chap. III ("The Modes of Meaning"), esp. p. 56.

3. See Alvin Plantinga, "De Essentia," *Grazer Philosophische Studien* 7/8 (1979); 101–21.

4. "World and Essence," in M. J. Loux, *Universals and Particulars* (Notre Dame, Ind.: Notre Dame University Press, 1976), pp. 369–70. Given (i) that Socrates has a haecceity and (ii) that he exists in a world other than the world that obtains, Plantinga can go on to argue, as he does, that if Socrates is snubnosed in *W*, then he is *necessarily* such that he is snubnosed in *W*. But if what I have said is correct, then it is not the case that individuals have such "world-indexed" properties necessarily. I don't exist in any worlds other than the world that obtains; the world that obtains is not necessarily such that I exist if it obtains; and I am not necessarily such that I exist in it.

5. I have tried to show this in detail in *The First Person* (Minneapolis and Brighton: University of Minnesota Press and Harvester Press, 1981), Chap. 6, and in "The Primacy of the Intentional," *Synthèse* (1984): 89–109.

6. Some philosophers have been unduly impressed by the fact that quantified modal logic happens to have been developed in such a way as to contain the theorem "$(x) N (x = x)$." The philosophical question is whether there is anything for this theorem to express other than the proposition that everything is self-identical.

6

Coming into Being
and Passing Away:
Can the Metaphysician Help?

What We Have a Right to Believe about Ourselves

I assume that, in our theoretical thinking, we should be guided by those propositions we presuppose in our ordinary activity. They are propositions we have a right to believe. Or, somewhat more exactly, they are propositions that should be regarded as innocent, epistemically, until there is positive reason for thinking them guilty.

A list of such propositions would be very much like the list of propositions with which G. E. Moore began his celebrated essay, "In Defence of Common Sense."[1] The list I might make for myself may be suggested by the following: "(1) I am now thinking such and such things and have such and such beliefs, feelings, and desires. I now see people, for example, and I don't see any unicorns. And I have thought such and such other things in the past and then had such and such other beliefs, feelings, and desires. (2) I now have a body of such and such a sort and I had a body of such and such a different sort in the past. And (3) I am now acting with the intention of bringing about such and such things—and I could instead have acted with the intention of bringing about such and such other things. In the past I have acted with the intention of bringing about such and such other things, and I could then have acted with the intention of bringing about such and such other things instead."

There is such a list that each of us might make. The items on the list are obvious and, one might think, so trivial as not to be worth mentioning at all. Yet some of those who now say that these things are trivially true may say, at the end, that strictly speaking they are false. But one can't have it both ways.

A sceptic may ask: "Might it not be that I'm mistaken in suggesting there are these things we know about ourselves? Isn't it possible that I'm deluded about these things?" Of course, it's *possible* that I am deluded about these things. It's *possible* that I will wake up in a few minutes and find myself in a hospital. But from the fact that it is thus theoretically possible that I am deluded it hardly follows that it is now reasonable for me to think that I am in fact deluded. Until you give me some very good positive reason to think the contrary, it is now reasonable for me to assume that I am in a room with other people and not suffering from hallucination or delusion.

These are some obvious truths about myself, then, which it is now reasonable for me to accept. But these truths, if we take them at their face value, imply that I am an *ens per se*, that is to say, they imply that, in the strictest sense of the word "is," there *is* a certain thing which is I.

Now some philosophers have held that the word "I" is a logical construction, a mere *façon de parler*, like the expressions "−5" and "the average plumber." One can *show* that "−5" and "the average plumber" are logical constructions. For one can take sentences in which these ostensible terms occur ("−5 is 7 less 2" and "the average plumber has 2.6 children") and translate them into other sentences no longer containing terms ostensibly referring to −5 and the average plumber. If I, too, am simply a logical construction, or *façon de parler*, then the various truths on the list that I have made could be reformulated without reference to me. They could be re-expressed in new sentences which contain no terms, such as the word "I", which ostensibly designate me. The new sentences might contain terms designating what I now call my sensations, as Ernst Mach and Bertrand Russell once thought, or they might contain terms designating my body or certain parts of my body, as other philosophers have thought. But these various philosophers do not *know* that the word "I" is thus a logical construction, a mere *façon de parler*. No one can take the sentences I have cited − the truisms about myself − and translate *them* without loss of meaning into sentences referring only to things other than me. If you think that I am mistaken about this, just consider the truth which I can now express by saying, "I don't see any unicorns," and try to put exactly what *that* says in sentences which don't refer to me.

Perhaps you will say on reflection: "Well, I can't do it now, but maybe some day somebody will do it." This would be like the sceptic we just considered. It's possible you can show I'm a mere *façon de parler*. And it's possible that I am now lying in a hospital bed somewhere. But what have these mere possibilities got to do with what is going on in fact? They certainly do not mean that I *am* deluded with respect to the truisms that I began. No one has been able to show that these truths can be paraphrased as truths about some entity or entities other than myself. And therefore no one has been able to show that I am not an *ens per se*.

I say, then, that we have a right to assume that persons are *entia per se*, that there *are* persons, in the strict and philosophical sense of the expression "there are." You and I, in short, are real things and the terms that designate us are not linguistic fictions. But if there *are* persons, in the strictest sense of the expression "there are," then persons are such that either (i) they exist forever or (ii) they come into being but will not pass away or (iii) they will pass away but never come into being or (iv) each is such that it came into being and will pass away. I assume that the last of these four possibilities is the one that is most likely. You and I exist now but there was a time before which we did not exist and there will be a time after which we will no longer exist.

We should be clear, at the outset, about one very simple point. The concepts of *coming into being* and *passing away* are not merely physiological concepts. Consider the relation, for example, between the concepts of *passing away* and *dying* and assume (what, of course, is doubtful) that the latter concept is pretty clearly fixed. If by "passing away," we mean, as I do, *ceasing to be*, then if we say that the body dies we cannot say that it passes away—for the body continues to exist but in such a way that it is no longer alive. It may well be that, when the body dies, then the person whose body it is passes away—that the person ceases to be. But the two concepts are different. It's *logically* possible that, when the person's body dies, then the person does *not* cease to be. And it's also *logically* possible that the person ceases to be *before* his body dies. To admit this distinction is not to say that there is any likelihood that these possibilities are actual. The point is only that it is one thing to say that a person's body has died and it is another thing to say that the person has ceased to be, even if in fact the two events coincide.

And, similarly, the concept of *coming into being* is not the same as any physiological concept. Conceivably there is some physiological event which coincides uniformly with the coming into being of a person, but to say that this physiological event occurs is not the same as saying that a person comes into being.

The points I have just made are typically philosophical. I know they will bring forth two quite different reactions. One reaction will be: "But why insist upon what is trivial and obvious?" And the other reaction will be: "What you say is obviously false." As long as there are people who react in the second way, and I know that there are such people, it is worthwhile to insist upon what is obvious, even if it is trivial. For, as Aristotle said, if you *deny* what is trivial, then there is no hope for your investigation.

Of course there may be philosophers or there may be people practicing medicine who don't think there are any persons. And this means, if they are consistent, that they don't believe with respect to themselves that they ever came into being or that they will ever pass away. For people who do really believe that, I have no message—except to urge them to think again.

Alteration

One of the ways in which a metaphysician can help a nonmetaphysician is to protect him from bad metaphysics.

People are sometimes led to think that nothing persists through any period of time and hence that all things are constantly ceasing to be and new things are constantly coming into being to replace them. This was the view of Heraclitus who said "You cannot step into the same river twice." (One of Heraclitus's followers, according to Aristotle, held that things are in such constant flux that you can't even step into the same river once.) If this view is true, then it would be incorrect to say that you and I have existed for any period of time. The things that bore our names at any given moment yesterday have since then ceased to be and you and I are no more the same people as those people of yesterday than we are identical with each other. This view is a disastrous beginning, if our aim is to understand coming into being and passing away.

Why would anyone think that such a thing is true? Respectable philosophers I regret to say, have accepted this view. When philosophers don't simply pick their theories out of the air, they arrive at them in attempting to deal with philosophical puzzles. The kind of puzzle that has led philosophers to think that everything is in flux, in the sense in question, may be illustrated as follows.

You say to me: "I see you have a new fence in your back yard." I say: "No, it's the same fence I've always had." You say: "But your fence is red; the fence you used to have was white." I say: "No, it's the *same* fence; I painted it, that's all." And you say: "But it *couldn't* be the same fence. If something A is identical with something B, then whatever is true of A is true of B. But if today's fence is identical with yesterday's, how can it be that the old one is red and the other is white?"

Very great philosophers, I'm afraid, have stumbled over that one. (Some have been led to conclude not that everything is in flux, but that things can be identical with each other even though they don't have all their properties in common.) What went wrong in the dialogue we have just imagined?

Consider the sentence: "Today's fence is red and yesterday's fence was white." One trouble with it is that the dates are in the wrong place. For what we know is not merely that there was something that was *yesterday's fence* and that was white. It is rather that there *is* something that is a fence and that was *white yesterday*. And it's not merely that there is a thing that is *today's fence* and is red. It's rather that there is a fence that is *red today*. The fence I have now and the fence I had yesterday have *all* their properties in common. I have had just one fence — one that is red today and that was white yesterday.

If you don't see the error involved in using the expressions "today's fence" and "yesterday's fence," perhaps this analogy will help. Consider someone who reasons as follows: "Mr. Jones the husband is very meek and submissive. Yet Mr. Jones the father is extremely authoritative and overbearing. But one and the same thing can't be meek and submissive and *also* authoritative and overbearing. Therefore there are two Mr. Joneses — Mr. Jones the husband and Mr. Jones the father."

Saying what went wrong in this case is like explaining a joke. But perhaps we should risk it. It's not that Mr. Jones the husband has properties that are different from those that Mr. Jones the father has. It's rather that Mr. Jones is such that he is meek and submissive toward his wife and overbearing and authoritative toward his children.

All this is to spell out, once again, what ought to be obvious. But let us keep the moral in mind: The fact that a thing has *altered* in a certain way does not imply that the thing has ceased to be and that some new thing has come into being.

Coming into Being and Passing Away
Secundum Quid

We are assuming, then, that persons—you and I—are real things, *entia realia*. And we are also assuming that they come into being and pass away. But this means that the coming into being and the passing away of persons is also the real thing. That is to say, it's not a pseudo kind of coming into being and passing away; it's not that kind of merely apparent coming into being and passing away that some of the Scholastics called coming into being and passing away *secundum quid*. Let us consider for a moment this pseudo kind of coming into being and passing away.

In his book *Generation and Corruption*, Aristotle considers a man who had a talent for music and who then lost this talent but continued to exist for some time thereafter. Aristotle described this fact by saying: "The musical man passed away and an unmusical man came to be, but the man persists as identically the same" (I, 4, 319b). One is inclined to ask: "Why on earth did Aristotle express himself *that* way? After all he was just talking about a certain alteration. Why didn't he say that a man *ceased to be musical*, instead of saying that a musical man *ceased to be*?"

It should be noted that we, too, sometimes talk that way. That is to say, we sometimes use such expressions as "coming into being" and "passing away" to describe what is in fact the mere alteration of a persisting subject. Thus you may ask me: "How is our old friend Jones?" And I may reply by saying: "The Jones you knew doesn't exist any more. He's just dull and bitter now." A reporter once wrote, after visiting one of our great comedians in a nursing home in California: "Alas, the great comedian is no more." But the man—the man who had been a comedian—persisted for some time after that.

It was a result of Aristotle's way of talking ("the musical man ceased to be") that medieval philosophers—St. Thomas, for example—came to distinguish between (1) coming into being and passing away *per se* and (2) coming into being and passing away *per accidens* or *secundum quid*.

We have coming into being *per accidens*, or *secundum quid*, when a thing alters in some way or other—when there is something which so changes that it first has a certain property and subsequently has a certain other property instead. This is what happens if a musical man is said to cease to be and an unmusical man to come into being when in fact one and the same man persists through the change.

Let us consider some other examples.

It is sometimes said that, when one becomes aware of a feeling or of a sensation, then the feeling or sensation is something that comes into being *ex nihilo*. When British and American philosophers, in the first third of the century, were concerned about the status of what they called appearances or sense-data, they took very seriously the possibility that these are things that come into being, *ex nihilo*, when the appropriate physiological and psychological conditions obtain.[2] But isn't the fact of the matter that, when a feeling or sensation is thus said to "come into being," what actually happens is that the person or subject is simply altered in a certain way? In making me feel sad, for example, what you do is not to cause a feeling of sadness to come into being *ex nihilo*, but to cause me to have a certain property—that of feeling in a certain way. An analogously for making me aware of an "appearance" or "sense-datum." What you do is simply to cause me to sense in a certain way. But if this is true, then the so-called coming into being and passing away of feelings and sensations is simply coming into being and passing away *per accidens* or *secundum quid*—and not coming into being and passing away *per se*.

Let us consider another type of case. One might say: "If I turn the light on over our heads, I will make a *shadow* come into being out of nothing. And if I then turn the light out again, I will cause the shadow to go out of existence—without leaving any traces behind. And so isn't this genuine coming into being and passing away—coming into being and passing away *per se*?"

I think the answer is no. But it is instructive to consider the case somewhat further. What we conveniently describe as a shadow coming into being and passing away can also be described, somewhat less conveniently, as an alteration in what we might call the shadowed object, or the shadowed objects. When I create a shadow on the floor, what I do is merely cause a certain part of the floor to be darker, to reflect less illumination than it had before. And when I make the shadow cease to be—to disappear without remainder—all that I do is to cause the relevant parts of the shadowed object to reflect light once again. So we don't have a coming into being and passing away *per se* of shadows. All we have is a coming into being and passing away *per accidens* or *secundum quid*—a mere alteration in the shadowed object.

Let us note that a shadow is a paradigm case of what some medieval philosophers called an *ens in alio*—and what we might call an "ontological parasite." *Entia in alio* were thought of as things that got all their being, so to speak, from *other* things. Thus a shadow has no being of its own. Anything we seem to be able to say about it is something that really is a truth just about some shadowed object or other. The shadow is entirely parasitical upon its object. And this is really to say that there aren't such things as shadows.

Whatever thus comes into being or passes away *secundum quid* is not a real thing; it is an ontological parasite, at best a mere *façon de parler*.

Sometimes we say that a certain thing x *became* a certain other thing y. And we take our statement to imply that the first thing x then ceased to be and the second thing y then came into being. In such a case, we are speaking of coming into being and passing away *secundum quid*; x and y are ontological parasites and not *entia per se*. This may be seen as follows.

If the first thing became the second thing, then we may say:

(1) There exists a z such that z once was x and z now is y.

Suppose now we add

(2) x has now ceased to be and y hadn't yet come into being when z was x.

If we taking "coming into being" and "passing away" literally and thus mean coming into being and passing away *per se*, then our two statements will imply

   (3) There exists a z such that (i) z was once identical with x, (ii) z is now identical with y, and (iii) x but not y no longer exists.

But (3) is absurd. Therefore, if (1) and (2) are true, they must be taken to refer to coming into being and passing away *secundum quid*. The fact of the matter was simply that z was altered in a certain way.

If at a certain time, a thing literally *becomes identical* with something it hadn't been identical with before, then the thing came into being at that time and it wasn't identical with anything before.[3]

Leibniz's Law implies that nothing can change its identity. That is to say, it is impossible for there to be anything that is identical with a certain thing at one time and diverse from that thing at another time. ("The G is diverse from the H," unlike "The G is such that it is not identical with the H," implies "There is something which is identical with the H.") For suppose that there is something, say, the G, that is identical with the H today and will be diverse from the H tomorrow. If the H is now identical with the G, then anything that is true of the G is also true of the H. Therefore if the G will be diverse from the H tomorrow, then the H will be diverse from the H tomorrow. But this consequence is absurd.

"Last year the President of the United States was identical with Mr. So-and-so. This year the President of the United States is identical with Mr. Such-and-such. And Mr. Such-and-such is diverse from Mr. So-and-so. Therefore things *can* change their identity and be identical at one time with what they are diverse from at another time."

Surely the argument does not merit refutation. If we restrict the use of "there is" to its strict and proper sense, we will not take the premises of the argument to imply that there *is* — or *was* — a certain thing x such that x was once identical with Mr. Reagan and x is now identical with Mr. Bush. *That* x is not even an *ens per accidens*.[4] Leibniz's law implies, then, that there cannot be substantial change. An individual thing or substance may come into being; it may be altered in various ways and it may pass away; but it cannot become *another* individual thing or substance.

Elanguescence

Reflection on the coming into being and passing away of sensations, feelings, and shadows may bring to mind a monstrous hypothesis proposed by Kant in the *Critique of Pure Reason*. Different things, he said, may have different *degrees of reality*. It is possible, he thought, for the degree of reality of a thing to increase or to decrease in a continuous manner. And so, he said, a thing "may be changed into nothing, not indeed by dissolution, but by gradual loss (*remissio*) of its powers, and so, if I may be permitted the use of the term, by elanguescence."[5]

Kant is to be taken literally here. He was clear that existence is not a predicate.

Yet he thought that some things could have *more* existence than others. It is as though he thought that there is a path between being and nonbeing, so that one day you may set out from nonbeing and head in the direction toward being with the result that the farther you go in that direction the more being you will have. But surely there is *no* mean between being and nonbeing. If something *is* on a certain path, then that something *is*. Or if it *isn't* yet, then it can't be on the path between being and nonbeing.[6]

Of course things may be more or less endowed. But things cannot be more or less endowed with respect to being. What is poorly endowed *is* poorly endowed and therefore *is*.

One might object: "Consider an intense pain that becomes less and less intense and finally fades away. Doesn't it become less and less real and thus gradually cease to be?" The objection would ignore the point we have just made about ceasing to be *secundum quid*. When we say that the pain gradually faded away, we are talking about the alteration of a person; we are speaking about the way in which a person felt or the way he experienced something. Thus one might say, similarly, that the feeling of sadness faded away and finally ceased to be altogether. But the fact of the matter is only this: a person felt less and less sad until he finally reached the point where he didn't feel sad at all. And we should remind ourselves, moreover, that even if we do reify pains and feelings of sadness, we have no ground whatever for saying that the feeling that is less intense is *less real* than the feeling that is more intense.

"But if one thing has more properties than another, isn't it more real than the other?" *No* thing has any more or any less properties than does any other thing. Every property and every thing is such that either the thing has that property or the thing has the negation of that property. If you can play the viola and I cannot, you don't have *more properties* thereby than I.

To be sure, you have the property of being someone who can play the viola and I don't have *that* property. But I have the property of being someone who cannot play the viola and *you* don't have that property.

Coming into Being and Passing Away *Per Se*

What, then, is the strict sense of coming into being and of passing away? I suggest the following tensed definitions:

D1 x comes into being = Df There is a property which is such that x has it, and there is no property which is such that x had it

D2 x has just passed away = Df Something that was such that x exists begins to be such that x does not exist

One question that was discussed at length by medieval philosophers is: "When a thing comes into being, does the thing exist — or is it the case merely that the thing is going to exist. And when it passes away, does the thing exist — or is it the case merely that the thing once existed.[7] These definitions presuppose that the thing exists when it comes into being and also that it exists when it passes away.

The Coming into Being and Passing Away of Persons

If persons are real things or *entia per se*, then the coming into being and passing away of persons is *not* a matter merely of something or other being *altered* in a certain way. When my body dies, then it is altered in a certain way. And if it happens to be the case that I then cease to be, as it well may be, then my ceasing to be is *not* just the fact that my body has been altered in a certain way. And when I came into being, this may well have been at the time of a certain alteration of the fetus, or of a certain alteration of matter that was going to become a part of the fetus. But whatever alteration that may have been, that alteration was not the same event as my coming into being. For our assumptions imply that persons are *entia per se* and not *entia in alio*—not ontological parasites like shadows.

What does all this have to do with the facts of biology and physiology, with the questions about when human life begins and ends? Not very much, I'm afraid. What I've said so far won't help anyone in dealing with *those* questions. But if you begin at the point at which I've begun, you will want to put the question first the other way around. What do the facts of biology and physiology, the things we know about the beginning and ending of human life, tell us about the coming into being and passing away of persons? Here, too, I'm afraid, the answer is not very much—or not very much as far as anyone can possibly know. But there may be some relevant points that the metaphysician can make.

The United States Supreme Court decreed, in the case of *Roe* v. *Wade*, in 1973, that the fetus before a certain stage of development is not a "person in the whole sense." Possibly the ruling presupposes Kant's absurd hypothesis about degrees of reality. Then it would be telling us that, in its fetal stage, the person is somewhere between being and not being ("On the one hand, it doesn't really exist, and on the other hand, it doesn't really not exist"). But it would be more charitable not to assume that the court was presupposing bad metaphysics. And it is more likely that the court meant only that becoming a human being is a gradual process: the fetus is on the way to becoming a human being but, at its early stages at any rate, hasn't gotten there yet. One could take a similar view about the process of ceasing to be a human being. The one who is moribund is gradually ceasing to be a human being; in the early stages of his illness he is still a human being, but in the later stages not.

This view has recently been set forth by Lawrence C. Becker in *Philosophy and Public Affairs*.[8] It may be summarized in the two theses: "Entry into the class of human beings is a process" and "Exit from the class of human beings is a process."[9] The expression "human being" is certainly a proper term of biology and physiology; one cannot quarrel with these theses on terminological grounds. But I am not at all convinced that this gradualistic theory, even if it is true, will help us very much in dealing with the philosophical and ethical questions involved in the coming into being and passing away of those things that may thus gradually become or cease to be human.

To see that these theses are probably not helpful, let us consider the consequence of assuming that they are true. We may do this by relating them to what we have already said.

Consider the process of becoming a human being. (As Professor Becker makes clear, much of what we can say about the process of becoming a human being can also be said, *mutatis mutandis*, about the process of ceasing to be a human being.) Let us consider this thesis, that entrance into the class of human beings is a gradual process, and take it together with what we have already assumed. Thus we have:

(1) I am one of the members of the class of human beings.

(2) There was a time at which I did not exist.

(3) Entrance into the class of human beings is a gradual process.

Let us now consider our three premises together. I am as certain as I am of anything that the first of these premises is true. And I don't think there are many of us who are prepared to challenge the second. The third premise is the statement of the biological hypothesis we are now considering.

Our premises, quite clearly, have these two consequences:

(4) There was a time at which I was not one of the members of the class of human beings.

(5) My entrance into the class of human beings was a gradual process.

The second of these consequences — "My entrance into the class of human beings was a gradual process" — may suggest the process of entering a room. If we consider a man who is entering a room, we may say that his entrance is gradual in this sense: it begins with the entrance of the front part of one of his feet and this is followed by the entrance of more and more parts of his body. Then, when he gets them all in, he has entered the room. But perhaps a more accurate figure would be that of a sober man who becomes drunk: his entry into the class of the people who are drunk might be thought to be gradual.

But consider this further consequence:

(6) There was a time at which I existed but had not yet entered the class of human beings.

If I went through the process of *becoming* a human being as (5) tells us, then I wasn't *already* a human being when I started to go through this process.

What (6) tells us can be rephrased this way:

(7) My coming into being antedated my entry into the class of human beings.

Consider Aristotle's conception of the musical man once again. Aristotle might have said: "A musical man came into being but the man himself had existed long before." And then he could have said that the man's coming into being antedated his entrance into the class of musicians. For the man can become more and more musical without thereby coming into being, just as a man can become more and more drunk without thereby coming into being. Analogously, one could say that I came to be more and more human but without thereby coming into being. In each case, the thing that went through the process of gradual entrance is assumed to have antedated that process.

This is a consequence, then, if we take what is obvious and combine it with the thesis that "entrance into the class of human beings is a process."

If entrance into the class of human beings is a process, then my coming into being antedated my entrance into the class of human beings. This means that the event that is my coming into being is not the *same* as that event which is my entrance into the class of human beings. There was a time, before I entered the class of human beings, when I existed. And so, if someone at that time could have caused me to cease to be, my ceasing to be as well as my coming into being would have antedated my entrance into the class of human beings.

If in the future someone causes me gradually to leave the class of human beings, then, while he's doing this, while I *am* gradually leaving the class of human beings, I will be there to make the exit, and the man will not yet have caused me to cease to be. When I'm half way out of the room, *I'm* somewhere, partly in the room, partly outside, and partly in the doorway. Perhaps, once you've gotten me all the way out of the class of human beings, then you will have caused me to cease to be. But I suppose no one knows.

Would it help if we replaced the concept of *entrance* by the pair of concepts, *full* and *partial* entrance? Then we could distinguish between *full* and *partial* entrance into the class of human beings. And we could also do this in the case of entering a room. As soon as I get a part of my body in the room, then, however small the part may be, I have partially entered the room. And it is not until I have all the parts of my body in the room that I can say that I have fully entered the room. But I don't think this will help. For if we replace "entrance" by the two concepts "full entrance" and "partial entrance," then we have to give up the process theory. One has only to reflect just a little to see that both partial and full entrance can only be instantaneous.[10]

I am certain, then, that this much is true: if I'm a real thing and not just a *façon de parler*, then neither my coming into being nor my passing away is a gradual process—however gradual may be my entrance into and my exit from the class of human beings.

Now if we give the biologist and physiologist the term "human," perhaps we have a right to use the term "person" for the sort of thing that you and I are. Suppose now we define *a person* in terms of what it *could* become. We might say, for example, that a person is a thing that is such that it is physically possible (it is not contrary to the laws of nature) that there is a time at which that thing consciously thinks.[11]

If we thus define a person—as that which is necessarily such that it is physically possible that there is a time at which it consciously thinks—then we cannot say that anything gradually becomes a person or gradually ceases to be a person. For if a thing has the property of being necessarily such that it is not contrary to the laws of nature that there is a time at which it consciously thinks, then it has that property from the moment it comes into being until the moment it passes away.[12] And so the questions we thought we escaped with our gradualistic concept of being a human may arise once again with the concept of a person.

The Moral of the Story

If all of this is right, as it seems to be, then no one could have known just when it was that I came into being. And no one will know just when it is that I will pass away. Or perhaps the latter point should be put more cautiously: the present state of our knowledge is such that, if I have the misfortune to be one of those people who, as Lucretius put it, "leave the light dying piecemeal," then no one will know just when it is that I will pass away.

Hence it *may* be, for all anyone knows, that by terminating my mother's pregnancy at a certain very early stage, one could have caused *me* then to cease to be. (But it may also be that I didn't come into being until after that stage.) And it *may* be, for all anyone knows, that, by disconnecting a life-sustaining device at a very late state in my gradual exit from the class of human beings, you will *then* cause me to cease to be. (But it may also be that I already ceased to be, sometime before that.)

Analogous things may be said about you and about everyone else.

So where does this leave us with respect to the moral problems that are involved in causing someone to cease to be? Surely it is right, sometimes, to terminate a pregnancy or to disconnect a life-sustaining device. Doubtless such acts always call for an excuse.[13] But let's not pretend that, when we perform them, probably we are not causing anyone to cease to be. Let's have the courage to face the moral facts of the matter: occasionally it *is* right for one person to annihilate another.

Notes

1. See G. E. Moore, *Philosophical Papers* (London: George Allen & Unwin, 1959), pp. 32–59.

2. Compare C. D. Broad's discussion of "Causation and Creation" in *Scientific Thought* (London: Kegan Paul, Trench, Trubner, 1925), pp.535–43.

3. Aristotle attempts to circumvent this conclusion with his doctrine of prime matter and substantial change. I cannot believe that he was successful. But I think it is clear that, if one does wish to circumvent this conclusion, then one must appeal to a concept that is very much like that of prime matter.

4. According to Aristotle, accidents cannot be transferred from one subject to another.

5. See the "Refutation of Mendelssohn's Proof of the Permanence of the Soul," in *Critique of Pure Reason*, B414; the passage appears on p. 373, of the Norman Smith translation (London: Macmillan, 1933). Compare also Kant's discussion of the "degrees of reality" in the "Anticipation of Perception," B207–9.

6. Compare the criticism of Kant's doctrine in Franz Brentano, *The Theory of Categories* (The Hague: Martinus Nijhoff, 1981), pp. 74–77.

7. If all beginnings are instantaneous, then no ending is instantaneous. For suppose (i) there was an instant at which Socrates ceased to be and (ii) an instant at which his survivors begin to be such that he no longer exists. Then either these instants are the same (in which case the instant is one at which Socrates both exists and does not exist) or the second instant is later than the first (in which case, since between any two instants there are other instants, Socrates would neither exist nor not exist during the intervening instants). But to say that there is thus no instant at which a thing passes away is *not* to say that the thing passes away gradually. See Norman Kretzmann, "Incipit/Desinit," in Paul K. Machamer and Robert G. Turnbull (eds.), *Motion and Time, Space and Matter* (Columbus: The Ohio State University Press, 1976), pp.101–36.

8. Lawrence C. Becker, "Human Being: The Boundaries of the Concept," *Philosophy and Public Affairs*, 4 (1975): 334–59. Compare W. R. Carter, "Do Zygotes Become People?" *Mind*, 91 (1982): 77–85.

9. Becker, "Human Being," 335, 336.

10. We can, of course, retain proposition (6) above—i.e., "There was a time at which I existed but had not yet entered the class of human beings"—if we replace "entered" by "fully entered." What if we replace it by "partially entered"? For all we know, the result might be a proposition that is false. It may be that, from the time I *did* come into being, whenever that was, I already had one foot in the door, so to speak, and was *part* way into the class of human beings.

11. The moral philosopher might insist upon defining a person as a thing having *rights* of a certain sort. If now we should give *him* the term "person," then we might appropriate the term "self" and consider our definition as a definition of *a self*.

12. And so we are saying more than that persons are things that are "potentially thinkers." For if we take "potential" in its ordinary sense, then we may say that our potentialities are variable and dependent on our circumstances at any particular time. But our potentialities, in this sense of the term, are a function of what it is physically possible for us to be—a function of what the laws of nature do not preclude us from being. And physical possibilities, in this latter sense, are invariable. I have attempted to distinguish these various senses of possibility in more detail in *Person and Object: A Metaphysical Study* (La Salle, Ill.: Open Court, 1933), Chap.2.

13. Can part of the excuse be that the persons involved aren't then humans in the complete sense? This moral question falls outside the scope of the present paper.

Part III
Parts and Wholes

7

Parts as Essential to Their Wholes

I

One kind of philosophical puzzlement arises when we have an apparent conflict of intuitions. If we are philosophers, we then try to show that the apparent conflict of intuitions is only an apparent conflict and not a real one. If we fail, we may have to say that what we took to be an apparent conflict of intuitions was in fact a conflict of apparent intuitions, and then we must decide which of the conflicting apparent intuitions is only an apparent intuition. But if we succeed, then both of the intuitions will be preserved. Since there was an apparent conflict, we will have to conclude that the formulation of at least one of the intuitions was defective. And though the formulation may be embedded in our ordinary language, we will have to say that, strictly and philosophically, a different formulation is to be preferred. But to make it clear that we are not rejecting the intuition we are reformulating, we must show systematically how to interpret the ordinary formulation into the philosophical one. The extent to which we can show this will be one mark of our success in dealing with the philosophical puzzle. Another will be the extent to which our proposed solution contributes to the solution of still other philosophical puzzles.

I shall consider a philosophical puzzle pertaining to the concepts of whole and part. The proper solution, I believe, will throw light on some of the most important questions of metaphysics.

The Presidential Address delivered at the twenty-fourth annual meeting of the Metaphysical Society of America, Tulane University, March 16, 1973.

II

The puzzle pertains to what I shall call the principle of mereological essentialism. The principle may be formulated by saying that, for any whole x, if x has y as one if its parts then y is part of x in every possible world in which x exists. The principle may also be put by saying that every whole has the parts that it has necessarily, or by saying that if y is part of x then the property of having y as one of its parts is essential to x. If the principle is true, then if y is ever part of x, y will be part of x as long as x exists.

Abelard held that "no thing has more or less parts at one time than at another."[1] Leibniz said, "We cannot say, speaking according to the great truth of things, that the same whole is preserved when a part is lost."[2] And G. E. Moore gave us this example:

> Let us take as an example the relational property which we assert to belong to a visual sense-datum when we say of it that it has another visual sense-datum as a spatial part: the assertion, for instance, with regard to a colored patch half of which is red and half yellow: "This whole patch contains this patch" (where "this patch" is a proper name for the red half). It is here, I think, quite plain that, in a perfectly clear and intelligible sense, we can say that any whole, which had not contained that red patch, could not have been identical with the whole in question: that from the proposition with regard to any term whatever that it does not contain that particular patch it *follows* that that term is other than the whole in question — though *not* necessarily that it is qualitatively different from it. That particular whole could not have existed without having that particular patch for a part. But . . . it seems quite clear that, though the whole could not have existed without having the red patch for a part, the red patch might perfectly well have existed without being part of that particular whole.[3]

Instead of considering such things as sense-data and visual patches, let us consider physical things. Let us picture to ourselves a very simple table, improvised from a stump and a board. Now one might have constructed a very similar table by using the same stump and a different board, or by using the same board and a different stump. But the only way of constructing precisely *that* table is to use that particular stump and that particular board. It would seem, therefore, that that particular table is *necessarily* made up of that particular stump and that particular board.

But to say of the table that it is necessarily made up of the stump and the board is not to say of the stump and the board that *they* are such that they are necessarily parts of the table. And it is not to say that the stump is necessarily joined with the board. God could have created the stump without creating the board; he could have created the board without creating the stump; and he could have created the stump and the board without creating the table. But he could not have created *that* particular table without using the stump and the board.

Let us be clear about the view that is here set forth. It is no spurious essentialism. (That is to say, it is not the kind of essentialism that is arrived at in such arguments as these: "Szigeti was a violinist; necessarily all violinists are musicians; therefore Szigeti was necessarily a musician"; and "The word 'Homer', as we use it, connotes or intends being a person who wrote the *Iliad* and the *Odyssey*; therefore Homer, if he existed, was such that he necessarily wrote the *Iliad* and the *Odyssey*.") We are saying, in application to our example of the table, that there exists and x, a y, and a z such that: x is identical with this table, y is identical with this stump, z is identical with this board, and x is such that, in every possible world in which x exists, it is made up of y and z. Our statement says nothing whatever about the way in which human beings may happen to conceive or to look upon such things as this table. And, a fortiori, it says nothing whatever about the way in which we may happen to describe this table or use the language we do. Its subject matter is no more nor less than this table, the parts of this table, and the possible worlds in which this table exists.

Considered in the abstract and considered in application to such simple examples as these, the principle of mereological essentialism may seem obvious. Indeed, I would say that it ought to seem obvious. Yet the principle appears to conflict with certain other truths that perhaps from a somewhat different point of view, would *also* seem to be obvious. I will indicate these other truths by formulating two objections to the principle of mereological essentialism.

(A) "(i) My automobile had parts last week that it does not have this week and it will have parts next week that it never had before. But (ii) the principle of mereological essentialism implies that, if anything is ever a part of my automobile, then that thing is a part of my automobile as long as the automobile exists. And therefore (iii) the principle of mereological essentialism is false."

(B) "(i) I could have bought different tires for my automobile. (ii) If I had bought different tires for my automobile, then it would have had different parts from those it has now. Therefore (iii) my automobile could have had different parts from those it has now. Hence (iv) my automobile is such that, in some possible worlds, it has parts it does not have in this one. But (v) the principle of mereological essentialism implies that in every world in which my automobile exists it has exactly the same parts it has in this one. And therefore (vi) the principle of mereological essentialism is false."

Philosophers who are interested in the ways in which people ordinarily talk may wish to multiply examples at this point. But I believe that our two examples are enough.

I would say, then, that we have here a typical philosophical puzzle—an apparent conflict of intuitions.

III

Before we try to solve the puzzle, let us consider the antithesis of extreme mereological essentialism. This would be what we might call complete, unbridled mereological *inessentialism*.

Complete, unbridled mereological inessentialism would seem to be manifestly absurd. This would be the view that, for any whole w, w could be made up of any two things whatever. For, given such a view, one could say, of *this table*, that it could have been made up of the number 36 and the property blue.

Perhaps it will be conceded that the set of things that are capable of being parts of this table must be restricted in at least a general way – say, to things of the same ontological category as the table. Suppose, then, one says that, for any two physical objects, this table could have been made up of those two objects.

If the view is true, then *this table*, this physical thing that is before us now, is such that it could have been made up of my left foot and the Grand Central Station. Or, to be more exact, if extreme mereological inessentialism is true, then this table, my left foot, and the Grand Central Station are three things that are such that there is a possible world in which the first is made up of the second and third – in which *this table* is made up of what, in this world, are my left foot and the Grand Central Station.

Indeed, there would be indefinitely many such possible worlds. In trying to imagine this table being made up of my foot and the station, perhaps we thought of my foot and the station as they now are, with all the particular parts that they now happen to have. But if extreme mereological inessentialism is true, then the foot and the station could have had parts entirely other than those that they have in fact. The foot could have been made up of Mt. Monadnock and Mr. Robinson's necktie and the station could have been made up of a certain horse and a certain fish. So, of the indefinitely many possible worlds in which this table is made up of the foot and the station, some of those will be such that in them the foot is made up of the mountain and the necktie while the station is made up of the horse and the fish, but others will be such that in them the station is made up of the horse and the necktie while the foot is made up of the mountain and the fish.

It is difficult to imagine how even God could tell these worlds apart. Which are the ones in which the necktie is made up of the horse and the station and which are the ones in which the mountain is made up of the fish and the foot? One would have to say, of the mountain and the necktie and the horse and the fish, that they could have been made up of other things, too. Hence, of those worlds in which the foot is made up of the mountain and the fish, there will be those in which the fish is made up of the necktie and the station. . . .

But we need not formulate such extreme examples. Consider just two tables, x and y, and suppose, what from one point of view would seem to be reasonable, that these tables are such that they could survive replacement of any of their smaller parts. We consider, then, the consequences of exchanging certain of their smaller parts; then there will be a world possible in respect to this one in which x has one of the parts that y has in this world and y has one of the parts that x has in this world; then there will be a world possible in respect to *that* world, and therefore also in respect to this one, in which x and y will have exchanged still other smaller parts. We can imagine the process continued in such a way that it will remind us of the ancient problems of The Ship of Theseus and The Carriage.

There will be a possible world that is like this one except for the fact that in that one x has the parts that y has in this one and y has the parts that x has in this one. We have only to reflect a moment to see that there will be indefinitely many such possible worlds. Thus of those possible worlds W, which are such that the thing u which is one of the legs of x in this world is the corresponding leg of y in W and the thing v which is one of the legs of y in this world is the corresponding leg of x in W, there will be those worlds W′ which are such that the things that are parts of u in this world will be parts of v in W′ and there will those worlds W″ which are such that the things that are parts of v in this world will be parts of u in W″, and so on, ad indefinitum.

These reflections, on the consequences of extreme mereological inessentialism, may suggest to us that *some* version of mereological essentialism must be true—even if it is not the extreme principle we have set forth. But instead of trying to formulate plausible alternatives to the extreme principle (a task which I have found to be extraordinarily difficult), let us return to our philosophical puzzle and see whether the extreme principle might not be defended.

IV

Let us begin by introducing some mereological definitions and axioms, taking as undefined "x is part of y" where "part" is understood in the sense sometimes expressed by "proper part." Now it is possible that the term "part" is taken in one way in our formulation of the principle of mereological essentialism and in another way in our formulation of the objections to it. In the principles that follow, we will use the term "S-part" instead of "part." Use of "S-part" will indicate that we are speaking strictly and philosophically. Then we may formulate, without ambiguity, certain questions about the relation of "part" in its ordinary, or loose and popular, sense, and "S-part" or "part" in its strict and philosophical sense.

Of the three axioms and the three definitions that follow, the first two in each group were set forth, though in a somewhat different terminology, by Whitehead in *The Organisation of Thought.*[4]

(A1) If x is an S-part of y and y is an S-part of z, then x is an S-part of z.

(A2) If x is an S-part of y, then y is not an S-part of x.

(A3) If x is an S-part of y, then y is such that in every possible world in which y exists x is an S-part of y

We are suggesting, then, that the principle of mereological essentialism be taken as a basic principle of the theory of part and whole. We add these definitions:

(D1) x is discrete from y = Df (i) x is other than y and (ii) there is no z such that z is an S-part of x and z is an S-part of y.

(D2) w is strictly made up of x and y = Df (i) x is an S-part of w, (ii) y is an S-part of w, (iii) x is discrete from y, and (iv) no S-part of w is discrete both from x and y.

(D3) x is strictly joined with y = Df There is a w such that w is strictly made up of x and y.

Making use of the above terminology and principles, as well as the concepts of spatial and temporal location, let us now consider the make-up of certain ordinary and familiar things.

V

Consider the history of a very simple table. On Monday it came into being when a certain thing A was joined with a certain other thing B. On Tuesday A was detached from B and C was joined to B, these things occurring in such a way that B remained throughout as a part of a table. And on Wednesday B was detached from C and D was joined with C, these things occurring in such a way that C remained throughout as a part of a table. Let us suppose that no other separating or joining occurred.

Mon	AB
Tue	BC
Wed	CD

I suggest that in this situation there are the following three wholes among others: AB, that is, the thing made up of A and B; BC, the thing made up of B and C; and CD, the thing made up of C and D. I will say that AB "constituted" our table on Monday, that BC "constituted" our table on Tuesday, and CD "constituted" our table of Wednesday. Although AB, BC, and CD are three different things, they all constitute the same table. We thus have an illustration of what Hume called "a succession of objects."[5]

One might also say, of each of the three wholes, AB, BC, and CD, that it "stands in for" or "does duty for" our table on one of the three successive days. Thus if we consider the spatial location of the three wholes, we see that on Monday AB occupied the same place that our table did, on Tuesday BC occupied the same place that our table did, and on Wednesday CD occupied the same place that our table did. And so we might define "constitutes" in the following way:

(D4) x constitutes y at t = Df There is a certain place such that x occupies that place at t and y occupies that place at t.

The final clause could also be read as "y occupies exactly that same place at t." We add this obvious definition:

(D5) x constitutes at t the same physical object that y constitutes at t′ = Df There is a z such that x constitutes z at t and y constitutes z at t′.

Every physical object will, of course, constitute itself. But, according to our present suggestion, some things may constitute, and be constituted by, things other than themselves. (Thus AB constituted our table on Monday; but AB, unlike our table, also ceased to be on Monday.)

What if our table should undergo fission with the result that on Thursday there

Mon	AB	
Tue	BC	
Wed	CD	
Thu	CE	EF

were two different tables, CE and EF? We cannot say that CE and EF *both* constitute the same table as does CD, BC, and AB. For our definitions imply that, if two different things constitute the same table at the same time, then those two things are in the same place at that time; and CE and EF are not in the same place on Thursday.

It is possible, however, that one or the other, CE or EF, constitutes the same table as does CD. Which one, then? To answer *this* question, we would have to turn to the philosophy of tables, or to the philosophy of furniture, and attempt to set forth *criteria* which a pair of things must satisfy if one of them at one time is to constitute the same table as does the other of them at another time. But this project is not relevant to our present discussion.

Similar remarks will apply to fusion—to what happens when two tables are joined to make a single table. The fused table will not constitute the same table as *both* of the original tables—but it may, or may not, constitute the same table as one of them.

And so we have described one possible way of looking upon what happens when, as we would ordinarily put it, a thing such as a table undergoes a change of parts. I propose that we consider our philosophical problem from this perspective. Before doing so, however, we should consider two objections to this way of looking at the matter.

(1) "You are committed to saying that AB, BC, CD and our table are four different things. It may well be, however, that each of the three things AB, BC, CD, satisfies the conditions of any acceptable definition of the term 'table'. Hence you are committed to saying that, in the situation described, there are *four* tables. But this is absurd; for actually you have described only *one* table."

We will find the answer, I think, if we distinguish the strict and philosophical sense of such expressions as "There are four tables" from their ordinary, or loose and popular, sense. To say that there are four tables, in the strict and philosophical sense, is to say that there are four different things, each of them a table. But from the fact that there are four tables, in this strict and philosophical sense, it will not follow that there are four tables in the ordinary, or loose and popular sense. For there to be four tables in the ordinary, or loose and popular, sense, it must be the case that there are four things, not only such that each constitutes a table, but also such that no two of them constitute the same table.

We may, therefore, explicate the ordinary, or loose and popular, sense of "There are *n* so-and-so's at t" in the following way:

(D6) There are, in the loose and popular sense, *n* so-and-so's at t = DF
There are *n* things each of which constitutes a so-and-so at t and no two of which constitute the same so-and-so at t.

The term "so-and-so" in this schematic definition may be replaced by any more specific count-term, e.g., "table" or "ship."

And so the answer to the above objection is this: In saying that there are four tables in the situation described one is speaking in the strict and philosophical sense and not in the loose and popular sense; and in saying that there is just one table one is speaking in the loose and popular sense and not in the strict and philosophical sense. The two assertions, therefore, are not incompatible.[6]

(2) The second objection to our way of looking at the simple table — or tables — above may be put as follows.

"You say that the thing constituting our table at a given time may be something *other* than the table itself. Yet you say that it occupies exactly the same place that the table does. Therefore what you say is incompatible with the principle according to which it is impossible for two things to occupy exactly the same place at the same time."

The expression "It is impossible for two things to be in the same place at the same time" may be taken either in a strict and philosophical sense or in a loose and popular sense.

If we take it in a strict and philosophical sense it tells us that it is impossible for there to be an x and a y such that x is diverse from y and x occupies at a certain time exactly the same place that y occupies at that time. If we take the principle in this sense, then we must say that it is false. For a shadow and a part of the surface of a physical object may occupy exactly the same place at the same time; so, too, for a hole in a shadow and a part of the surface of an object; so, too, perhaps, for a person and a part of his body; and so, too, for any two things one of which constitutes the other. Thus the AB of our example is other than the persisting table x; yet on Monday AB occupies the place that x does; but in so doing AB does not get into the way of x, for on Monday it is AB that does duty, so to speak, for x. Hence it is no objection to say that our way of viewing the table is incompatible with the strict and philosophical sense of the principle, "It is impossible for two things to be in the same place at the same time."

And what we have said is not incompatible with the loose and popular sense of the principle. Taken in that sense, the principle tells us that it is impossible for there to be two physical objects, in the loose and popular sense of "There are two physical objects," occupying the same place at the same time. What we have said does not imply that there are two physical objects, in this loose and popular sense, occupying the same place at the same time. Looking back to D6, we see that there cannot be two physical objects in this sense unless there are two physical objects neither of which constitutes the other.

VI

We are now in a position to reply to the two objections to our version of mereological essentialism.

The first objection was this: (A) "(i) My automobile had parts last week that it does not have this week and it will have parts next week that it has never had before. But (ii) the principle of mereological essentialism implies that, if anything is ever a part of my automobile, then that thing is a part of my automobile as long as the automobile exists. And therefore (iii) the principle of mereological essentialism is false."

In reply to this objection one may observe that the term "part" is used in one way in the first premise and in another way in the second and hence that the conclusion rests upon an equivocation. But if the reply is to be taken seriously, one must state what the two uses of the term "part" are and how they are related to each other.

In formulating the principle of mereological essentialism, we used the expression "S-part," suggesting that this might be read as "part in the strict and philosophical sense." (Perhaps the reader would prefer to read it as "part in the philosopher's sense.") We proposed three axioms in the attempt to explicate "S-part." This is the sense in which "part" should be taken in premise (ii) of the above objection.

What of premise (i)? Here, I suggest, "part" must be taken in the loose and popular sense. (Perhaps the reader would prefer to say: "Here 'part' must be taken in its ordinary sense.") How, then, are we to relate this loose and popular sense of "part" to the strict and philosophical concept of S-part?

To say, for example, that a certain tire is now a part of my automobile is to say that what now constitutes that tire is a part, in the strict and philosophical sense, of what now constitutes my automobile. And to say of a certain other tire that it was a part of my automobile yesterday is to say that something that constituted that tire yesterday was a part of something that constituted my automobile yesterday. I propose, then, this definition of the ordinary sense of "part" in terms of the vocabulary we have here introduced:

(D7) x has y as a part at t = Df Something that constitutes y at t is an S-part of something that constitutes x at t.

Taking "part" in this ordinary, or loose and popular sense, we may now say of a physical thing, such as my automobile, that it may have one part at one time and another part at another time. And saying this will be quite consistent with saying, as our principle of mereological essentialism requires us to say, that in a strict and philosophical sense if a thing y is ever a part of a thing x then that thing y is a part of x at any time that x exists.

The second objection was this:

"(B) (i) I could have bought different tires for my automobile. (ii) If I had bought different tires for my automobile, then it would have had different parts from those it now has. Therefore (iii) my automobile could have had different parts from those it has now. Hence (iv) my automobile is such that, in some possible worlds, it has parts it does not have in this one. But (v) the principle of mereological essentialism implies that in every world in which my automobile it has exactly the same parts it has in this one. And therefore (vi) the principle of mereological essentialism is false."

Here, too, we may observe that the term "part" is used equivocally — in the loose and popular sense in premises (ii) and (iii) and in the strict and philosophical sense in premise (v). But now we must show how the "could have" of premises (ii) and (iii) is to be explicated in the strict and philosophical vocabulary. And when we have done that, we may consider the status of premise (iv) — the premise according to which my automobile is such that in some possible worlds it has parts it does not have in this one.

The statement, "My automobile could now have a certain thing as one of its parts," even when restricted to its ordinary or loose and popular sense, has a certain ambiguity. On the one hand, it could be taken in a somewhat narrow sense to mean the same as (A) "My automobile could have O as one of its parts and remain an automobile while having O as a part." One the other hand, it could be taken more broadly to mean the same as (B) "My automobile could become a thing that has O as a part," where there is no implication that the thing which is my automobile remains an automobile after it has taken on O as a part. Let us define "x could have y as a part of t" in this second, broader sense. For given this broader sense of "could" one can then readily express in terms of it what is intended by the narrow sense (in our example, "x is an automobile and x could be at t an automobile having O as a part").

If something w is strictly made up of two things x and y, then x is strictly joined with y (see D2 and D3). Our principles imply that, in such a case, w is necessarily such that it has x as a part, in the strict and philosophical sense of the term "part." But they do not imply that x is necessarily such that it is a part of w. And they do not imply that x is necessarily such that it is joined with y. Returning to our very simple table which, we supposed, was strictly made up of a stump and a board, we may recall that, although the table is necessarily such that it has the stump as a part, in the strict and philosophical sense of the term "part," the stump is not necessarily such that it is a part of the table and it is not necessarily such that it is joined to the board.

To say, then, in the loose and popular sense, that my automobile could now be a thing having a certain tire will be to say that something that now constitutes a part of my automobile could be joined with something that now constitutes the tire.

Let us say, then:

(D8) x could have y as a part at t = Df There is a w and a v such that (i) w is an S-part of something that constitutes x at t, (ii) there is a time at which v constitutes y, and (iii) there is a possible world in which w is strictly joined with v.

If we say, then, in this loose and popular sense, that my automobile could have a certain tire as one of its parts, we are *not* saying that there is a possible world in which that automobile does have that tire as one of its parts. We are saying, rather, that something that constitutes a part of my automobile and something that constitutes the tire are such that there is a possible world in which *they* are joined together.

And so now we see that the fourth proposition in our objection does not follow from the second and third. From that fact that my automobile *could*, in this loose and popular sense, have a certain tire as a part, it does not follow that my automobile is such that in some possible world *it* has that tire as a part.

If, for any reason, we should persuade ourselves that this table could have been made up of my left foot and the Grand Central Station, we need not be led to the infinity of indiscernible possible worlds discussed earlier. We need not suppose that, in some of the worlds in which this table is made up of the foot and the station, some are such that the foot is made up of the mountain and the horse and others are such that it is made up of the necktie and the fish. For we may say what we like about the possible makeup of the table, the foot, and the station, without committing ourselves to the thesis that any of these things exist in any possible world other than this one.

The theory of possibility does not require us to say, of any of these common sense objects — the automobile, the table, the station, the mountain, the horse, the foot, the necktie, and the fish — that they exist in any other possible worlds. But it does require us to say, of the strict and philosophical wholes that constitute these commonsense objects, that *they* exist in other possible worlds.

This last point, however, must be put more precisely.

VII

Let us consider two ordinary tables, x and y, that evolved in the way depicted

	x	y
Mon	AB	CD
Tue	BC	DE
Wed	CD	EB
Thu	DF	AB

on the accompanying diagram. We are supposing that on Monday there were two things, each of them a table, one made up of A and B and constituting x, and the other made up of C and D and constituting y; that these two things "evolved" into BC and DE, respectively, on Tuesday, then on Wednesday into CD and EB, and finally on Thursday into DF and AB. We will suppose further that no additional joinings or separatings took place.

Our present question is: can we put precisely the difference between the two kinds of things that are here involved — the difference between such things as x and y on the one hand and such things as AB, BC, CD on the other?

It is tempting to say that the ordinary or vulgar things, x and y, differ from the strict and philosophical things AB, BC, and CD in that, whereas the ordinary things are constituted by different things at different times, the philosophical things are never constituted by different things at different times. We cannot say this, however, although we will say something very much like it.

The relation of constituting, as we have defined it in D4, is symmetrical. Hence, not only does AB constitute x on Monday, but x also constitutes AB on

Monday. But AB constitutes y on Thursday and therefore y constitutes AB on Thursday. Therefore the philosophical object like the vulgar object is constituted by different things at different times.

Let us say that our diagram depicts two *object series* — where the term "object series" is an alternative for Hume's "succession of related objects." An object series will be a set of objects related to each other as the constituents of our ordinary table x are related to each other and as the constituents of the ordinary table y are related to each other. The mark of an object series will be that it is a set of things related by succession: AB was succeeded by BC, BC was succeeded by CD, and so on. But instead of saying that the individual thing AB was succeeded by the individual thing CD, let us think of succession as relating *sets* of things. We will say that the set consisting of AB and Monday was succeeded by the set consisting of BC and Tuesday; and so on. (Thus, although we might be able to say that the individual thing CD was succeeded by DE on Tuesday and by DF on Thursday, we cannot say anything comparable of the set consisting of CD and Monday.) We will introduce, then, the concept of an *object-pair*.

(D9)   C is an object-pair = Df C is a class containing just a thing and a time such that the thing constitutes an object during the time.

In this definition and in those that follow, the term "object" may be replaced throughout by any count-term — for example, "table" or "ship."

Let us introduce the notation "[x,t]" as an abbreviation for the locution "the object-pair having as members the individual thing x and the time t."

To define succession, we first define *direct succession*, construing the latter concept in such a way that: [BC,Tue] directly succeeds [AB,Mon]; [CD,Wed] directly succeeds [BC,Tue]; and [DF,Thu] directly succeeds [CD,Wed]. We will also be able to say that: [DE,Tue] directly succeeds [CD,Mon]; [EB,Wed] directly succeeds [DE,Tue]; and [AB,Thu] directly succeeds [EB,Wed]. Each object-pair may also be said to be its own direct successor. Direct succession is not otherwise exemplified in the things depicted in our diagram. I propose this definition:

(D10)   [x,t] is a direct object successor of [y,t′] = Df (i) t does not begin before t′; (ii) x constitutes at t the same object that y constitutes at t′; and (iii) either x is identical with y, or there is a z such that z is an S-part of x, z is an S-part of y, and at any time between t and t′ inclusive there is some w that then constitutes the same object that y constitutes at t′, and z is an S-part of w.

Our definition enables us to say, then, that [BC,Tue] is a direct object successor of [AB,Mon]. Or, replacing "object" in our definition by "table" throughout, we may say that [BC,Tue] is a direct table successor of [AB,Mon]. The definition assures us that B persisted throughout the period from Monday to Tuesday and that, at all times within that period, B was an S-part of a table — an S-part of something that constitutes the same table that AB constituted on Monday.

We should note that, given our definition, we may say of any object-pair that it directly succeeds itself. And this will be true not only of direct succession, but of succession more generally.

Of the "table-pairs" depicted in the x column of our diagram, the Wednesday and Thursday pairs were not *direct* successors of the Monday pair, but they were *successors* of the Monday pair, just as the Thursday pair was a successor of the Tuesday pair. Similarly for the table-pairs depicted in the y column. Succession is related to direct succession in the following way: u is a successor of v, if and only if, it is true either that u is a direct successor of v, or u is a direct successor of a direct successor of a direct successor of v, or u is a direct successor of a direct successor of v, or . . . and so on. Hence we may define "successor" in the way that was suggested by Frege. Let us say:

(D11) [x,t] is an object successor of [y,t'] = Df t does not begin before t';
and (ii) [x,t] belong to every class C which contains [y,t'] and everything that is a direct object successor of any member of C

We may now say, of each of the "table pairs" depicted in our two columns, that it is a "table successor" of itself and of each of the "table pairs" depicted above it in the column.

Our two columns may be said to depict two "table series"—if we think of x and y as coming into being on Monday and as ceasing to be on Thursday. The more general concept of "object series" may be defined this way:

(D12) C is an object series = Df C is a class having as its members an object-pair x, all the object successors of x, everything of which x is an object successor, and nothing which is unrelated to x by object succession.

The final clause is, of course, short for: "nothing which is such that neither it is an object successor of x nor x is an object successor of it." Hence, any two members of an object series will be such that one of them succeeds the other. We add this definition:

(D13) C is an object series corresponding to x = Df C is an object series, and every member of C contains a thing and a time such that that thing constitutes x at that time

If x should pass away and then come into being again at a later time (assuming for the moment that this is possible) then there will be more than one object series corresponding to x.

We are now in a position to state the difference between ordinary things such as x and y, on the one hand, and the stricter things such as AB, BC, CD, on the

	x	y
Mon	AB	CD
Tue	BC	DE
Wed	CD	EB
Thu	DF	AB

other. We have noted that it is not enough to say that, whereas the ordinary things are constituted at different times by different things, the stricter things are always constituted (when they exist) by the same thing. For the ordinary things are always constituted (when they exist) by themselves, and the stricter things may be constituted at different times by different things — as the stricter thing AB is constituted by x on Monday and by y on Thursday, and the stricter thing CD is constituted by y on Monday and by x on Wednesday. But we may now characterize the difference between the two types of thing by reference to their corresponding object-series.

The object-series corresponding to the stricter things will be more constant than those corresponding to the ordinary things. Let us call the stricter things *primary objects* and define the concept as follows, by reference to the constancy of object-series:

> (D14) z is a primary object = Df No object-series corresponding to z has two members which are such that nothing belongs to both and z belongs to neither

Thus neither the x nor the y of our diagram is a primary object. The object series corresponding to x has at least two members — e.g., [AB,Mon] and [BC,Tue] — which are such that nothing belongs to both and x belongs to neither. Similarly for y.

But AB, BC, CD, DF, and EB will be primary objects. It is true that AB is constituted by x on Monday and by y on Thursday. But [x,Mon] and [y,Thu] are not members of the same object series; for neither one is a successor of the other. Analogously for CD and [y,Mon] and [x,Wed].

The S-parts of AB, BC, CD, DF, DE, and EB will also be primary objects. For any S-part of a primary object is itself a primary object.

Consider now the following objection to what has been said. "You say that, in the strict and philosophical sense, there were two different tables in one and the same place on Monday — one of them, AB, which ceased to be when A was disjoined from B, and the other of them, x, which was constituted by BC on Tuesday and by CD on Wednesday and which, therefore, persisted for at least three days. Now suppose that the world had been destroyed late on Monday. Would there still have been two tables — AB and x? Or would there have been just one? And if the latter, which one?"

In describing the situation, we supposed that there occurred no joinings or disjoinings other than the ones that were mentioned. Hence the situation involved three primary tables and one nonprimary table. Had the world been destroyed late on Monday, then the situation would have involved just one primary table and no nonprimary one. In short, there would have been just table AB and no table x. "Does your answer imply, then, that x did not come into being until Tuesday?" No, for a nonprimary object comes into being with the earliest members of its object pairs. And if an object pair is such that it is going to have a direct object successor which is other than it is, then the thing which belongs to it constitutes an object which is other than w. "But had there been just AB and no x on Monday, then our table would not have been such that it could have had parts other than those that it does have. For, on your account, only nonprimary objects are such that they could have parts which are other than they do have." The latter assertion is mistaken, Given D8, our definition of "x could have y as a part at t," we may say, in the loose and popular sense of "part," that primary objects are such that they could have parts other than those they have in fact, even though, in the strict and philosophical sense of "part," in the sense we have expressed by the term "S-part," they have exactly the same parts in every possible world in which they exist.

According to the principle of mereological essentialism if a thing loses any of its parts, then it ceases to be. In describing the history of table x, we said that on Tuesday A was detached from B. This means, therefore, that AB ceased to be on Tuesday. But now we find that what constitutes y on Thursday is an object made up of A and B. Is this the same AB as the one that constituted x on Monday or is it a different one? I have assumed that it is the same AB—and, more generally, that if a primary object u is made up of the same things as is a primary object v, then u is identical with v.

What I have just said, however, is contrary to the opinion of Thomas Reid, who argues as follows: "I see evidently that identity supposes an uninterrupted continuance of existence. That which hath ceased to exist, cannot be the same with that which afterwards begins to exist; for this would be to suppose a being to exist after it ceased to exist, and to have had existence before it was produced, which are manifest contradictions."[7] But it seems clear to me that the propositions in question are *not* manifest contradictions. It would be contradictory to suppose a being to exist after it had ceased to exist *for the last time*, and to have had existence before it was produced *for the first time*. But these things are not what we are supposing when we say that a thing can come into being after it has ceased to be.

We may now put more precisely the point that was formulated above as follows: "The theory of possibility does not require us to say, of any of these commonsense objects—the automobile, the table, the station, the mountain, the horse, the neckties, and the fish—that they exist in any other possible worlds. But it does require us to say, of the strict and philosophical wholes that constitute these common sense objects, that *they* exist in other possible worlds."

The theory of possibility does not require us to say of any *nonprimary* object that it exists in any possible world other than this one. But it does require us to say that *primary* objects exist in possible worlds other than this one. What we can truly say about the unrealized possibilities of nonprimary things may be reformulated more precisely in terms of the unrealized possibilities of primary things. We do not need to suppose, therefore, that there are possible worlds which are indiscernable except for the fact that some nonprimary things are constituted by one set of primary things in one of them and by another set in another. And what we say is entirely compatible with the principle of mereological essentialism: if x has y as one of its parts, in the strict and philosophical sense of the term "part," then in every possible world in which x exists, x has y as one of its parts.

VIII

Finally, let us note briefly how these suggestions relate to certain other philosophical questions and puzzles.

(1) Consider first what has been called "the Paradox of Increase." "It is impossible for anything to increase by the addition of parts, since when further parts are adjoined to a thing, neither that to which the parts are adjoined, nor the adjoined parts themselves, increase in the sense that they have more parts than they had before. . . . What then can be made of the way in which both ordinary usage and logic appear to countenance increase?"[8]

We think we can make things bigger just by adding parts to things. But what *are* the things that we then make bigger? Suppose we have a certain thing A and then attach to it a certain other thing B. We then have a bigger object than we had before (assuming that neither A nor B shrunk or contracted during the process). But what object *became* bigger? It was not either A or B, for both of these remained the same size they were before. And it was not AB for AB did not exist until A was joined with B. That is to say, AB did not have two different sizes, a smaller one at one time and a larger one at another.

If, in the situation I have described, there is something that became bigger, then there is something which was constituted by A or by B at one time and by AB at a later time and the thing that constituted it at the later time is bigger than the thing that constituted it at the earlier time.

(2) Consider secondly a puzzle about identity.

"Suppose that on Monday we cast a certain bar of metal into a statue. Then on Tuesday we melt the statue down and recast the metal into a vase. And on Wednesday we melt the vase and are left with just the piece of metal. Surely the statue *was* the piece of metal on Monday and the vase *was* the piece of metal on Tuesday. But the vase was not the statue and neither one of these was the piece of metal on Wednesday. Therefore we must say either that one and the same thing can be identical with one thing at one time and with another thing at another time or else that two things can be identical with the same thing. But both of these conclusions are absurd."[9]

Both of the conclusions are, of course, absurd. But if we describe the situation accurately, we will not be led to either. Thus we may say that what constituted the statue on Monday was identical with what constituted the piece of metal on Monday, that what constituted the vase on Tuesday was identical with what constituted the piece of metal on Tuesday but not with what constituted the statue on Monday, and that what constituted the piece of metal on Wednesday constituted neither the statue nor the vase on Wednesday. From the fact that the piece of metal and the statue constituted each other on Monday, we may not infer that they were identical with each other on Monday. For x is not identical with y unless x and y constitute each other during the entire time that either x or y exists. The statue, therefore, was not identical with the vase and neither of these was identical with the piece of metal.

"But if the statue was other than the piece of metal, then two different physical objects — the statue and the piece of metal — both occupied the same place on Monday. And that is impossible."

From the fact that the statue is other than the piece of metal and that they both occupied the same place on Monday, it does not follow that two different physical objects occupied the same place on Monday. For to say that two different physical objects both occupy the same place on Monday would be to say that there are two things, neither of which constitute the same object on Monday, and both of which are in the same place. See D6.

One could also deal with the problem, of course, by denying that there were two things, a vase and a statue, in addition to the piece of metal. One could say that there was just the piece of metal which had the property of being statuesque on Monday and that of being vase-shaped on Thursday. But if we allow tables and automobiles to count as things that come into being and pass away, why not also vases and statues? The view that has been proposed here does allow us to say that there are the three things in the situation described.

Indeed, we could revive the traditional term *mode* and say that the statue and the vase were at different times modes of the piece of metal. A thing x could be called a mere *mode* of a thing y provided only (i) x is necessarily such that everything that constitutes it at any time also constitutes y at that time and (ii) y is not necessarily such that what constitutes it at any time also constitutes x at that time.

Notes

1. See D. P. Henry, *Medieval Logic and Metaphysics* (London: Hutchinson University Library, 1962), p. 120.

2. *New Essays concerning Human Understanding*, Book II, Chap. xxvii, Sec. 11 (Open Court ed., p. 247). Compare Hume, *Treatise of Human Nature*, Book I, Part 4, Sec. 6.

3. *Philosophical Studies* (London: Kegan Paul, Trench, Trubner, 1922), pp. 287–88. Compare also J. M. E. McTaggart: "For if a whole is a combination it is built up of parts which could exist without being combined in that way, while the combination could not exist without them." *Some Dogmas of Religion* (London: Edward Arnold, 1906), p. 108.

4. *The Organisation of Thought* (London: Williams and Norgate, 1917), pp.158–62. Whitehead adds another axiom, to the effect that, if x is part of y, then there is a z such that z is part of x. Whitehead applies his theory of part and whole to *events*. I believe it is accurate to say that he conceives events in such a way that they may be said to have their parts necessarily.

5. See *A Treatise of Human Nature*, Book I, Part 4, Sec. 6 (Selby-Bigge ed., p. 255): "all objects, to which we ascribe identity, without observing their invariableness and uninterruptedness, are such as consist of a succession of related objects." In this same section, Hume affirms a version of the principle of mereological essentialism.

6. It may be noted that we have defined the loose and popular sense of the expression, "There are *n* so-and-so's at t" and not the more general, "The number of so-and-so's that there ever will have been in *n*." For the loose and popular sense of this latter expression is not sufficiently fixed to be explicated in any strict and philosophical sense. The following example may make this clear. In the infantry of the United States Army during World War II each private carried materials for half a tent — something like one piece of canvas, a pole, and ropes. Two privates could then assemble their materials and create a tent which would be disassembled in the morning. On another night the two privates might find different tent companions. Occasionally when the company was in camp the various tent parts were collected, stored away, and then reissued but with no attempt to assign particular

parts to their former holders. Supposing, to simplify the matter considerably, that all the tents that there ever will have been were those that were created by the members of a certain infantry company, how, making use of our ordinary criteria, would we go about answering the question "Just how many tents *have* there been?" Would an accounting of the history of the joinings of the various tent parts be sufficient to give us the answer?

7. Thomas Reid, *Essays on the Intellectual Powers of Man*, Essay III, Chap. 4. Compare Locke's *Essay*, Book I, Chap. 27, Sec.1: "one thing cannot have two beginnings of existence."

8. D. P. Henry, *Medieval Logic*, p. 120.

9. A slightly different version of this puzzle is set forth by Hugh Chandler in "Essence and Accident." *Analysis*, 26 (1966): 185–88.

8

Boundaries

Introduction

Stephan Körner has noted that one way of drawing up a theory of categories will divide all particulars "into (a) a class of independent particulars, i.e., particulars that are ontologically fundamental, and (b) a class of dependent particulars, i.e., particulars that are not ontologically fundamental."[1] The dependent particulars might be said to be "parasitical upon" the fundamental particulars.

I shall here discuss the nature of spatial boundaries, viewing them as dependent particulars.

What Are Boundaries?

Frege observes: "One often calls the equator an imaginary (*gedachte*) line, but it would be wrong to call it a line that has merely been thought up (*erdacht*). It was not created by thought as the result of a psychological process, but is only apprehended or grasped by thought. If its being apprehended were a matter of its coming into being, then we could not say anything positive about the equator for any time prior to this supposed coming into being."[2] Suarez had said, of the outer surfaces of a body, that they are genuine entities distinct from the body itself. And evidently he held that God could preserve the boundaries of a thing in separation from the thing (and also that God could preserve the thing in separation from its boundaries).[3]

Are boundaries parts of things? To avoid a mere verbal question, we will introduce the word "constituent" and say that things may have two types of constituent — parts and boundaries. And we will say that a part of a thing is a constituent which is not a boundary.

Why assume, then, that there *are* boundaries? The concept is needed for the description of physical *continuity*.

Contiguity and Continuity

What is it for two things to be continuous with each other?

Let us recall an ancient problem. "Consider two discrete physical bodies thought to be continuous with each other; the east side of body A, say, is continuous with the west side of body B. How is this possible? Either (i) the eastmost part of A is in the same place as is the westmost part of B or (ii) no part of A occupies the same place as does any part of B. In the case of (i), we would have two discrete things in the same place. But this is impossible. In the case of (ii), since A and B occupy different places, there is a place between the place where A is and the place where B is. But if there is a place between A and B, then A and B are not continuous."

Shall we say that, if two things are continuous with each other, then nothing can be put between them unless at least one of the two things is moved? This would be true, but it is too broad to capture the concept of continuity. For it holds of things that are merely *contiguous* with each other but which are not *continuous* with each other (for example, two blocks pushed together). A similar objection applies to the suggestion that, if two bodies are continuous with each other, then there is no space between them.

The problem requires that we make reference to the *boundaries* of things. Aristotle had said:

> The *continuous* is a species of the contiguous. I call two things continuous when the limits of each, with which they touch and by which they are kept together, become one and the same, so that plainly the continuous is found in the things out of which a unity naturally arises in virtue of their contact.[4]

If the continuous object is cut in half, then does the one boundary become two boundaries, one thing thus becoming two things? This is suggested by the passage from Aristotle. But how can one thing—even if it is only a boundary—become two things. And does this mean that when two things become continuous, then two things that had been diverse *become identical with each other*, two things thus becoming one thing?

Or should we say that when two things become continuous, then one of the outer boundaries ceases to be—*in nihilum*. This view has been attributed to Bolzano.[5] If we took this view, then we would have to say, of the thing that is cut in half, that one of the two severed halves keeps the boundary and that a new boundary comes into being which is then the boundary of the other half. This would seem to be a clear case of coming into being *ex nihilo*. And what is to determine which half gets the new boundary and which half keeps the old one?

Or could it be that one of the halves retains the old boundary and the other half is open-ended, having a side without a boundary—though not a side that is boundless? But what determines which side is to be the one without the boundary? If it is possible for a thing to exist without a boundary, why assume that either half has a boundary? And why assume that there is a boundary separating the two halves of the continuous object?

Or could it be that, if two things are in contact, then their boundaries *coincide* or overlap? Descartes, in speaking of the relation between a surrounding body and the body that it surrounds, speaks of "the common surface which is a surface that is not a part of one body rather than of the other."[6] This would mean that distinct boundaries can occupy precisely the same place at the same time. And it would also mean that, strictly speaking, more than one straight line can be extended between two points. This is the view that Brentano suggests.

Let us try to develop the suggestion further.

Boundaries, Parts, and Constituents

We will make use of the concepts of *constituent*, of *de re* necessity and of *coincidence*.[7] We presuppose that there is no actual concrete infinite—and hence that there cannot be lines that are infinitely long or bodies that extend infinitely in space. The expression "x is discrete from y" is an abbreviation for "there is nothing that is a constituent both of x and y."

There are two ways of defining *boundary*. We could appeal to the fact that a boundary is a dependent particular—a thing which is necessarily such that it is a constituent of something. Or we could appeal to the fact that a boundary is a thing that is capable of coinciding with something that is discrete from it. One of these should be a definition and the other an axiom.

Let us take the first course and say that a boundary is a dependent particular:

D1 x is a boundary in y =Df x is a constituent of y; and every constituent of
     x is necessarily such that there is something of which it is a constituent

Why not say simply that a boundary is a thing which is necessarily such that it is a constituent of something? In such a case, we would have to count as a boundary such a hybrid object as the sum or heap consisting of Venus and the top surface of a certain table.

It should be noted that we have defined "x is a boundary *in* y," and not "x is a boundary *of* y." The latter expression would normally be taken in such a way that it applies only to the outer boundaries of y. Thus, the expression "x bounds y" would normally be taken to abbreviate "x is a boundary of y." Any boundary *in* y is a boundary *of* a proper part of y.[8]

I have said, following Brentano, that the concept of a boundary is closely related to that of *total coincidence*. I suggest that the relation is this:

A1 For every x, x is a boundary, if and only if, x is possibly such that there
    is something with which it wholly coincides.

We will consider the logic of total coincidence below.

If we take as our primitive concept, that of being a (proper) *constituent*, then, as I have noted, we may define the concept of a (proper) *part* as follows:

D2 x is a part of y = Df x is a constituent of y; and x is not a boundary in y

If we replace "constituent" for "part" in the usual axioms for the concept of (proper) part, we can retain the axioms of transitivity and irreflexivity, as well as that of mereological essentialism (for every x and y, if x is a constituent of y, then y is necessarily such that x is a constituent of it). But although we can say that every part has a (proper) part, we cannot say that every constituent has a (proper) constituent. For a point may be a constituent without having a constituent.

The following axiom reflects the fact that boundaries are essentially dependent entities:

A2 For every x, y and z, if x is a boundary in y, and if z is a part of y in which x is not a boundary, then there is a part of y discrete from z in which x is a boundary

This principle implies that every constituent of every boundary is a constituent of something that is not a boundary. It is thus inconsistent with Suarez' suggestion, referred to above, according to which God could remove just the surface of a three dimensional object. The principle does not preclude our saying that there are hybrid objects such as the sum of Venus and a certain surface which is not a surface of Venus; but it does imply that, if there are such objects, then there are individual things which are discrete from such objects.

Could God preserve any of the boundaries of a thing apart from the thing? We could say that, for any thing having boundaries, God could destroy the thing and preserve the boundaries—by destroying some part of the thing such that the part did not contain any of those boundaries. But he couldn't preserve the boundaries except by retaining *some* part of the original thing.

Coincidence

We have taken as primitive the concept of *total coincidence*. Let us now express this concept by "x wholly coincides with y" ("xWy").

One axiom for this locution is A1 above:

A1 For every x, x is a boundary, if and only if, x is possibly such that there is something with which it wholly coincides

In formulating additional axioms, we will use the abbreviations: "xCy" ("x is a constituent of y"); "xDy" ("x is discrete from y") and "xBy" ("x is a boundary in y").

The relation of total coincidence is symmetrical and irreflexive:

A1.1 xWy → yWx

A1.2 xWy. → □(xWx)

Hence "xWy" is not transitive. But if one thing wholly coincides with a second thing and if the second thing wholly coincides with still a *third* thing, then the first thing wholly coincides with the third thing. In other words:

[xWy & yWz & □(x = z)] → xWz

We may also affirm that, if x wholly coincides with y, then every constituent of x wholly coincides with a constituent of y:

A1.3 xWy → {(z) (zCx) → [(Ev)(vCy & vWz)]}

And if two boundaries wholly coincide, then they are constituents, respectively, of two things having no *parts* in common:

A1.4 xWy → [(Eu) (Ev) (uDv & xBu & yBv)]

Total coincidence may hold between surfaces, or between lines, or between points, but it may not hold between two things of different dimensions or between solids. In terms of the undefined concept of total coincidence, we may now define the broader concept of coincidence:

D3 x coincides with y = Df either (a) x wholly coincides either with y or with a constituent of y or (b) a constituent of x wholly coincides with a constituent of y

The first clause of this definition insures that coincidence, unlike total coincidence, may obtain between points and lines, between points and surfaces, and between lines and surfaces; the second clause insures that coincidence — but not total coincidence — may obtain between three-dimensional things.

What, then, of dimensionality?

Dimensionality

We now define dimensionality — assuming that things may have either no spatial dimensions, or one such dimension, or two, or three. Thus we take it to be a necessary truth that there are exactly three spatial dimensions.[9]

We will not equate solids with what is 3-dimensional. That sum consisting of Venus and the top surface of the table is 3-dimensional, but not a solid. We will say, analogously, that there are no "broken surfaces"; hence that 2-dimensional object which is the sum of the front and back surfaces of a certain cube will not be a surface. And analogously there will be no "broken lines." Surfaces are like solids and unlike lines in that they may have holes.

We now set forth the following definitions:

D4 x is 0-dimensional (a point) = Df x is a boundary and x has no constituents

D5 x is 3-dimensional (a point) = Df x has constituents and is not a boundary

We have thus defined O-dimensionality and 3-dimensionality. Let us now consider 2-dimensionality.[10]

Shall we say that a 2-dimensional object is a boundary which is possibly such that the only things of which it is a constituent are 3-dimensional? No; for, if there cannot be things that are infinitely extended, then any part of the surface of a thing must also be a part of that 2-dimensional sum composed of it and some other part of the surface of the thing.[11] Thus the front surface of a cube must be a part of that 2-dimensional sum consisting of its front surface and back surface. Our conception of coincidence, moreover, requires that solids have "inner surfaces"; hence the entire outer surface of a solid is necessarily such that it is a constituent of 2-dimensional wholes consisting of it and an inner surface.

The concept of coincidence, however, presents us with one feature that is peculiar to 2-dimensional boundaries. A point is capable of coinciding with any number of points at a time; and a line is capable of coinciding with any number of lines at a time; but a surface can coincide only with one surface at a time. Let us say, then:

D6 x is 2-dimensional = Df x is a boundary; and for all y and for all z, if x wholly coincides with y and x wholly coincides with z, then y = z

(This definition, as well as the others here, should be taken to be in the present tense. If the definitions are interpreted "tenselessly", then a temporal variable should be taken to be implicit throughout.)

And now we may define 1-dimensionality:

D7 x is 1-dimensional = Df x is neither O-dimensional, 2-dimensional nor 3-dimensional; and x is necessarily such that it is a (proper) constituent of something that is 2-dimensional

Continuity

Two three-dimensional things are said to be discrete when they have no parts in common. It is convenient to introduce analogous concepts for 2-dimensional things and for 1-dimensional things. And so let us distinguish among three subspecies of discreteness: as a relation between 3-dimensional things; as a relation between 2-dimensional things; and as a relation between 1-dimensional things.

D8 x and y are 3-dimensionally discrete = Df x and y are 3-dimensional; and nothing 3-dimensional is a part of both

D9 x and y are 2-dimensionally discrete = Df x and y are 2-dimensional; and nothing 2-dimensional is a constituent of both

D10 x and y are 1-dimensionally discrete = Df x and y are 1-dimensional; and x is other than y

We may now distinguish three types of contact: that between 3-dimensional things ("touching"); that between 2-dimensional things; and that between 1-dimensional things.

D11 x is in 3-dimensional contact with y (x touches y) = Df is 3-dimensionally discrete from y; and x coincides with y

D12 x is in 2-dimensional contact with y = Df x is 2-dimensionally discrete from y; and x coincides with y

D13 x is in 1-dimensional contact with y = Df x is 1-dimensionally discrete from y; and x coincides with y

We may say, then, that a thing x is *in contact with* a thing y, provided only that x is either in 1-dimensional, 2-dimensional or 3-dimensional contact with y. And now we may say that x is *continuous* with y, provided only that x is in contact with y.[12]

Notes

1. Stephan Körner, *Categorial Frameworks* (Oxford: Basil Blackwell, 1970), p.4.

2. Gottlob Frege, *Foundations of Arithmetic* (Oxford: Basil Blackwell, 1950), p.35.

3. See Hugo Bergmann, *Das Philosophische Werk Bernard Bolzano* (Halle: Max Niemeyer, 1909), p. 207. Bergmann refers to Suarez's *Metaphysicae Disputationes*, XL, 5, Secs. 37 and 41.

4. Aristotle, *Metaphysics*, 1069a.

5. Compare Bernard Bolzano, *Paradoxes of the Infinite* (New Haven: Yale University Press, 1950). See paragraph 67 (p. 168). Bolzano speaks here of certain things but not others "being devoid of limiting atoms."

6. Descartes, *Principles of Philosophy*, Part 2, Principle XV; in E. S. Haldane and R. T. Ross, *Philosophical Works of Descartes*, vol. 1 (Cambridge: Cambridge University Press, 1931), p. 261.

7. The concept of coincidence is used by Franz Brentano, in Stephan Körner and Roderick M. Chisholm (eds.), *Philosophische Untersuchungen zu Raum, Zeit und Kontinuum* (Hamburg: Felix Meiner Verlag, 1976). Compare also Brentano's *Psychology from an Empirical Standpoint* (London: Routledge & Kegan Paul, 1973), pp. 351–58; *Psychologie vom empirischen Standpunkt*, Band II (Hamburg: Felix Meiner Verlag, 1971), pp. 259–62.

8. Brentano discusses inner and outer boundaries, *Raum, Zeit und Kontinuum*, p. 15.

9. One can, of course, construe time as a "fourth dimension." But it is not a fourth *spatial* dimension. The "four dimensional" things that relativity theory speaks about are *events* of a certain sort—not *bodies* having four spatial dimensions.

10. Brentano discusses dimension in *Philosophische Untersuchungen zu Raum, Zeit und Kontinuum*, pp. 13–16. He appears to assume, mistakenly, that the only boundaries found in surfaces are lines (but smaller surfaces will also be boundaries *in* any surface); and analogously for lines and points.

11. This point was made by Michael Zimmerman.

12. I am indebted to Stephan Körner, who introduced me to this topic when we were preparing Brentano's *Philosophische Untersuchungen zu Raum, Zeit und Kontinuum* for publication. I am also indebted to Robert Frederick, Richard Potter, James Van Cleve, and Michael Zimmerman.

9

Scattered Objects

I

The classic paper on scattered objects was written by Richard Cartwright.[1] What I present here may be thought of as a commentary on that paper. Like Cartwright, I believe that there are scattered material objects. But my views differ from his in several respects: (1) Where Cartwright makes use of such absolute spatial concepts as *point* and *region*, I make use of the relational concept of *touching* (or *direct spatial contact*). This alternative approach may throw a different light on some of the metaphysical questions that the problem of scattered objects involves. (2) I consider a distinction between two fundamentally different types of scattered objects—a distinction that Cartwright does not discuss. (3) I express some doubts about the relevance of "temporal parts" to the metaphysical problems that scattered objects involve.

II

I take the relation of *proper part of* (written henceforth as "part of") as undefined and assume that it is transitive and assymmetric:

(A1) For every x, y, and z, if x is part of y and if y is part of z, then x is part of z.

(A2) For every x, if x is part of y, then y is not part of x.

To abbreviate a further principle, I add two further definitions:

(D1) x is discrete from y = Df (a) x is other than y and (b) there is no z such that z is part of x and z is part of y.

(Without the first clause we would have to say of points and monads that they are discrete from themselves.)

(D2) x is composed of y and z = Df (a) y is part of x, (b) z is part of x, (c) y is discrete from z, and (d) no part of x is discrete from both y and z.

(This definition was first proposed by Whitehead.[2]) Consider a table of the following sort: It has a top T; it has four legs, A, B, C, and D; and it has no part that is discrete from each of the parts, A, B, C, D, and T. What is the table composed of? The question has many answers. We may say that it is composed of A and $TBCD$, also that it is composed of B and $TACD$, that it is composed of C and $TABD$, and that it is composed of D and $TABC$. (I use the locution "WX" as short for "that object that is composed of W and X" and "$WXYZ$" as short for "that object that is composed of WX and YZ.") If there are scattered objects, we may also say that the table is composed of T and $ABCD$, that it is composed of TA and BCD, that it is composed of $TABC$ and D, and that it is composed of such entities as the lower half of B and the remainder of the table.

III

We may define the concept of a scattered object if we allow ourselves the additional concept of *touching*, or *direct spatial contact*. (If a book is on the table and the table is on a rug, then, although the book may be said in some sense to be in spatial contact with the rug, it is not in *direct* spatial contact with the rug.)

(D3) x is a scattered object = Df there is a y and there is a z such that (a) x is composed of y and z and (b) no part of y is in direct spatial contact with any part of z.

The present sense of "scattered," it should be noted, does not preclude the possibility of *order*. "Scattered," therefore, should not be taken to imply "haphazard," "chance," or "random." The essential mark of a scattered object is the absence of a certain type of spatial contact.

IV

"Is there a material object composed of the Eiffel Tower and the Old North Church?"[3] If there is such a material object, then, we may agree, there are scattered material objects.

As Cartwright notes (p. 155), such entities as the following would seem to be quite respectable ontologically: the United States, the solar system, a suite of furniture, a pile of coal, a watch that is spread out on the watch repairer's workbench, printed words, the lowercase letters i and j, the constellation Cassiopeia.

But there are two extreme views about the existence of such objects.

One, which we could call conjunctivism, is the view that for any two individual things there is a third thing that is composed of both.[4] (Or we could qualify the doctrine by saying: "For any two individual things that are discrete from each other, there is a third thing composed of both.")

The other extreme could be put this way: All genuine individuals are *compact*; that is, they are nonscattered.

Sometimes the defender of the second view seems to presuppose the contradictory of that view. S/He may say: "Scattered objects are mere heaps or aggregates; and mere heaps or aggregates are not genuine things." This way of talking seems to imply that there *are* mere heaps or aggregates — and that such things are not "genuine." But if there *are* mere heaps or aggregates and if scattered objects are mere heaps or aggregates, then there are scattered objects.[5]

Consider again the example of Cassiopeia. One might argue as follows: Those particular stars have just been associated by human beings; other creatures might have associated some other group of stars — say, some group of stars that has never in fact been thought of as a constellation — and they might have called that constellation "Alcibiades." Now surely there *is* no constellation Alcibiades. But by similar reasoning there really is no constellation Cassiopeia.

The objection says, correctly, that we focused on Cassiopeia and not on that other group of stars that could have been called "Alcibiades." But the only relevant difference between the two heaps of stars is that we did focus on the former and not on the latter. The heap that might have been called "Alcibiades," unlike Cassiopeia, has no name in our astronomy, and therefore we do not call it a constellation. (If one insists that, although there is a heap, the constituent stars "do not form a constellation," then one is using "constellation" to mean a "heap of stars for which we have a name.").

V

Cartwright makes it abundantly clear that scattered objects play an essential role in the problem of identity through time.

Consider a whole W that persists through time — taking on new parts and shedding old ones during the course of its existence: I have depicted "the Ship of Theseus" in the following way:

		W	
Mon	X Y Z	[ABC]	
Tue	X Y	[ABZ]	C
Wed	X	[AYZ]	B C
Thur		[XYZ]	A B C

Column W depicts some of the parts that constituted Theseus on the four days Monday, Tuesday, Wednesday, and Thursday. The letters immediately to the left of the column depict parts of the flotsam that were later to constitute the ship of Theseus. And the letters to the right depict parts of the jetsam that was composed of the discarded part of Theseus.

The diagram could also be taken to depict a human body. Let us consider it that way and replace W by "Charlie." In doing this, we will be using the name

"Charlie" to refer to the type of thing that Cartwright used it for—an individual thing that may lose some of its parts and take on others.

If we look at our diagram, we can find a number of objects that are of a very different nature from Charlie. One of them is that object having parts *A*, *B*, and *C*, which occupied the place of Charlie on Monday. Let us call this object "Harry," thus using a name that Cartwright introduces at a similar point.

Consider the relations between Charlie and Harry. We can say, as Cartwright would, (1) that Harry and Charlie occupy exactly the same place on Monday, (2) that Harry is not identical with Charlie, and (3) that things never "change their identities" (roughly, you cannot be diverse from something today and identical with it tomorrow). Charlie and Harry are intimately related, then, but not identical. What more can we say about the relations between them?

I assume that Cartwright would want to say of *our* Charlie and Harry what he says of *his* Charlie and Harry:

> We have treated Charlie as a continuant, an object that endures for a period of time during which it undergoes change. It would seem only fair to treat Harry in the same way. Like Charlie, Harry underwent a certain change. He occupied a connected receptacle at *t* [Monday] and a disconnected one at *t'* [Thursday]. ("Scattered Objects," p. 166)

I believe that, in proposing to treat Harry "as a continuant" like Charlie, Cartwright supposes that, like Charlie, Harry is capable of losing parts—he says that *his* Harry *does* lose certain parts (see p. 169). But is it fair to our Harry to treat him this way? If Harry is that object that has parts *A*, *B*, and *C* and that occupies the place that Charlie occupies on Monday, doesn't Harry exist with precisely the *same* parts on the next three days? He becomes somewhat scattered on Tuesday, more widely scattered on Wednesday, and still more widely scattered on Thursday when he becomes a mass of jetsam.

Charlie—the human body occupying Harry's place on Monday—changed parts several times during the period depicted. But Harry did not change any parts at all. Indeed, Harry's parts would seem to be essential to him. Unless some of his parts cease to be in nihilum, it looks as though Harry will exist forever. What kind of a thing is he, then?

We might define the concept of a *substance* this way:

(D4) *x* is an individual substance = Df If *x* has parts, then for every *y*, if *y* is part of *x*, *x* is necessarily such that *y* is part of it.

The definition is put as it is to allow for the possibility that a monad is a substance. It also allows us to say, with Platonists, that abstract objects are substances (but this defect, if it is a defect, is easily remedied).

Those individuals that may survive the loss of their parts may be called *non-substantive individuals*. (I hesitate to use "nonsubstantial individuals.") Thus the Ship of Theseus and Charlie are nonsubstantive individuals. The metaphysical problem that Cartwright discusses in terms of what he calls the fusion principle now becomes, What is the relation between nonsubstantive individuals and substances?

By our definition, Harry is a substance and Charlie is not. And so we are left with the metaphysical question, What is the relation between Charlie and Harry?

VI

Cartwright introduces the philosophical concept of a *temporal part* at this point. He suggests that

> although Charlie and Harry are distinct objects, as is revealed by their divergent careers, a certain temporal part of Charlie is identical with a certain temporal part of Harry: Charlie's *t*-stage [Monday-stage], as we might call it, is identical with Harry's *t* stage. ("Scattered Objects," p. 169)

What *are* temporal parts, and what is the reason for thinking that such things as Charlie and Harry *have* temporal parts?

If we take "temporal part" in the technical sense in which, I believe, Cartwright understands it, then it will not do to say merely that a temporal part of a thing is a part that the thing has at a certain time and fails to have at other times, for some parts of the latter sort may be shed and then taken on again ("Let's try it once more with the old carburetor"). A temporal part, however, cannot be taken on again once it has been shed; whatever has it is necessarily such that it has it only once.[6]

There is a reasonably clear sense in which such entities as *states, processes,* or *careers* may be said to have temporal parts — parts that are unique to the times at which they are had and that cannot be taken on and off. Your second year and your twentieth year are different temporal parts of your life history. But our problem has to do with *individual things* and not with processes, states, or careers of individual things.

The question is, Why assume that individual things — such things as people, chairs, and matchboxes — have temporal parts? The assumption does give us a kind of answer to our metaphysical question about Harry and Charlie, but this fact does not seem to me to be by itself a sufficient reason for thinking that the assumption is true. Is there some other reason for thinking that it is true?

Evidently it is useful in theoretical physics to abstract from individual things and to investigate those processes that are the histories of such things. Hence physics may be said to investigate things that *do* have temporal parts. But it hardly follows from this that individual things have temporal parts.

To be sure, there are "process"-philosophers who say that such things as human bodies and matchbooks are really processes. But, so far as I know, no one has ever devoted any philosophical toil to showing how to *reduce* such things to processes. In the absence of such a reduction, I would agree with Broad, whom Cartwright quotes: "It is plainly contrary to common sense to say that the phases in the history of a thing are parts of the thing."[7] Harry is an individual who once had the shape and size of a man, but no process or career can have the shape and size of a man.

Could we modify Cartwright's suggestion, then, and say something similar to "a certain temporal part of Charlie's history is identical with a certain temporal part of Harry's history"? This seems to me to leave us with our problem. How are Charlie and Harry related if *they* are diverse and such that parts of their *histories* overlap?

I feel, therefore, that the appeal to temporal parts will not help.

Harry seems to make out better than he ought to. And, strangely, the one whose status is now unclear is Charlie. I am not really satisfied with any of the proposed solutions to the problem.[8] And so I hope very much that Cartwright will continue to work on it.

Notes

I am indebted to Judith Jarvis Thomson for a number of helpful suggestions.

1. Richard Cartwright, "Scattered Objects," in Keith Lehrer (ed.), *Analysis and Metaphysics*, (Dordrecht: Reidel, 1975); reprinted in Richard Cartwright, *Philosophical Essays* (Cambridge, Mass.: MIT Press, 1987). All references to Cartwright are to this paper.

2. A. N. Whitehead, *The Organization of Thought* (London: Williams and Norgate, 1917). p. 165. Whitehead used "separated from," whereas I have used "discrete from."

3. Cartwright, "Scattered Objects." p. 155.

4. S. Lesniewski proposed as an axiom of mereology: "For every non-empty class A of individuals there exists exactly one individual x which is a sum of all the members of A." And he said that an individual x is the *sum* of the members of a class A provided only that every member of A is a part of x and that no part of x is discrete from every member of A. See the exposition of Lésniewski's mereology in A. Tarski, *Logic, Semantics, Metamathematics*, (Oxford: Clarendon Press, 1956), pp. 24–29.

5. Compare Cartwright, "Scattered Objects," 158–59.

6. Compare Rudolf Carnap, *Introduction to Logic and Its Applications* (New York: Dover, 1958), pp. 197–210.

7. C. D. Broad, *An Examination of McTaggart's Philosophy*, vol. 1 (Cambridge: The University Press, 1933), pp. 349–50. Quoted by Cartwright in "Scattered Objects," p. 171.

8. My own most recent attempt to deal with the problem may be found in Radu G. Bogdan (ed.), *Profiles: Roderick M. Chisholm* (Dordrecht: Reidel, 1986), pp. 65–77. I suggest there that I may resemble Harry more than I do Charlie.

Part IV
The Mental

10

The Nature of the Psychological

I shall here formulate a definition of a *psychological attribute*. What I will say presupposes the common sense distinction between the psychological, or mental, and the nonpsychological.

The following may be taken as being paradigmatic cases of psychological attributes: judging; being sad about something; being pleased about something; wondering about something; feeling depressed; seeming to oneself to have a headache; and being appeared to redly. And the following will be paradigmatic cases of nonpsychological attributes: being extended; wearing a hat; being green; weighing 7 pounds; being the successor of 9; being such that all men are mortal.

There is a simple formula that tells us what the psychological attributes we have listed have in common and what distinguishes them from everything that is nonpsychological. It is this:

Any property which is possibly such that it is exemplified by just one thing and which includes every property it implies or involves is psychological

This formula provides us with an interpretation of one traditional thesis — namely, that whatever is 'purely qualitative' is psychological. We will *define* the psychological by reference to that which is purely qualitative. But we will not define the psychological *as* that which is purely qualitative, since certain psychological attributes — for example, thinking about one's brother — are not purely qualitative.

I will make the following metaphysical presuppositions. (1) It is necessarily the case that there are entities that are not individual things; examples are such abstract objects as propositions, attributes and numbers. (2) The ontological the-

Philosophical Studies 43 (1983) 155–164. *Copyright © 1983 by D. Reidel Publishing Co., Dordrecht, Holland, and Boston, U.S.A.*

sis of materialism ("Every individual thing is a material thing"), even if it is true, is not *necessarily* true. And (3) whatever is a proper part *has* a proper part.

These presuppositions seem to me to be clearly true, but it is not the point of the present paper to defend them. It is enough to note that, without them, our analysis of the psychological would have to be considerably more complex.

Our first task is to explicate the four expressions we have used in the formula above: 'property', 'implies', 'includes' and 'involves'. In doing this, I shall make use of four philosophical concepts. These are: (1) the concept of an *individual thing*; (2) the concept of *exemplification* at a time (as in '*x* exemplifies *y* at *t*' or '*x* has *y* at *t*'); (3) the concept of *de re modality* (as in '*x* is necessarily such that it is *F*'); and, finally, (4) the intentional concept of *conceiving* (as in '*x* conceives the property being red').

Properties

Let us think of an *attribute* as being anything that is capable of being exemplified:

D1 *P* is an attribute = Df. *p* is possibly such that there is something that exemplifies it.

I assume that there *are* attributes and that some of them are exemplified and others not. I also assume that every attribute is capable of being conceived – i.e., that every attribute is possibly such that there is someone who conceives it.

I will next single out a certain subspecies of attribute I will call a 'property'. This use of 'property' is entirely arbitrary; it is introduced only to avoid circumlocution. The definition of property will be so formulated that each of the psychological attributes on our list above will count as properties. The definition is this:

D2 *P* is a property = Df. *P* is an attribute which is such that: (a) only individual things can have it; (b) anything that can have it can have it, or fail to have it, at any time it exists; and (c) it can be such that some individuals have it and some do not.

Condition (a) tells us that if an attribute may be exemplified by a nonindividual (say, by an attribute or by a number), then that attribute is not a property. Hence being an even number and being exemplified are not properties. And no attribute that is capable of being universal is a property.

Condition (b) tells us that if *P* is a property, then whatever can have it can have it, or fail to have it, at any period of its existence – that is to say, at the time at which the thing comes into being and at any time thereafter up to and including the time it passes away. Hence coming into being and passing away will not themselves be properties. And what we might call 'past-tensed attributes' (for example, *being such that it did walk*) and 'future tensed attributes' (for example, *being such that it will walk*) will not be properties.

All the psychological attributes on our list above, as I have said, are *properties*, in the present sense of the term.

Implication and Inclusion

We have now explicated one of the four terms that appear in our general formula. We turn to *implication* and *inclusion*.

D3 *P* implies *Q* = Df. *P* is necessarily such that if anything has it then something has *Q*.

The attribute of being a man implies the attribute of being rational. And the attribute of being a person who owns a boat implies the attribute of being a boat. Inclusion in a subspecies of implication:

D4 *P* includes *Q* = Df. *P* is necessarily such that whatever has it has *Q*.

If *P* includes *Q*, then *P* also implies *Q*. But *P* may imply *Q* without including *Q*. The attribute of being a person who owns a boat implies but does not include the attribute of being a boat. And the attribute of being populated implies but does not include the attribute of being a living thing.

Nonrelational Properties

There is one noteworthy feature that has been traditionally associated with psychological or mental properties. It is that of being *internal* or *nonrelational*.

We are now in a position to specify one sense in which certain psychological properties may thus be said to be 'nonrelational'. For one mark of a *relational* property is this: a relational property implies a property it does not include. (Note I have said "implies a *property* it does not include".) The property of being a biped will be relational according to this account, since it implies but does not include the property of being a foot. But the property of being angry will be nonrelational; it includes every property that it implies. So, too, for the psychological properties with which we began: judging; being sad about something; being pleased about something; wondering about something; feeling depressed; seeming to oneself to have a headache; and being appeared to redly.

To be sure, judging implies but does not include the attribute of *being judged about* or that of *being an object of judgement*; and wondering implies but does not include the attribute of *being wondered about* or that of *being an object of wonder*. But being judged about and being wondered about are not *properties*, in our restricted sense of this term. They may be exemplified by such entities as propositions, attributes and numbers; hence they are not such that only individual things can have them. ("What, then, of *being an individual that is judged about*? No abstract object can have *that* attribute." This is true; but that attribute, unlike our psychological attributes, implies a property that it does not include—namely, that of judging.)

Psychological properties, however, are not the only properties that are nonrelational by our definition. The properties on the following list are both nonpsychological and nonrelational:

being either angry or two-legged;
being intoxicating;
being potentially dangerous;
being an individual thing that is nongreen.

But these attributes, unlike our paradigmatic psychological attributes, are all such that they *involve* properties they do not imply.

Involvement

What, then, is the requisite sense of involvement? Consider these four attributes: (i) *being either red or round*, (ii) *being nonred*, (iii) *being possibly red* and (iv) *wanting something that is red*. These attributes all *involve* the property red, yet they do not include or imply it.

Using the intentional expression 'conceives', we can say exactly what the requisite sense of 'involvement' is. Each of the attributes may be said in the following sense to *involve* the property red: the attribute is such that one cannot *conceive* it without conceiving the property red.

So let us define involvement this way:

D5 *P* involves *Q* = Df. *P* is necessarily such that whoever conceives it conceives *Q*.

We may note, incidentally, that these concepts of inclusion and involvement yield an identity condition for attributes:

An attribute *P* is *identical* with an attribute *Q*, if and only if: *P* includes *Q*, *Q* includes *P*, *P* involves *Q*, and *Q* involves *P*.

In other words: an attribute *P* is identical with an attribute *Q*, if and only if, they are necessarily such that (i) whatever has the one has the other and (ii) whoever conceives the one conceives the other. Hence attributes that imply and include each other need not be identical. *Being an equilateral triangle* and *being an equiangular triangle* are distinct attributes, since neither involves the other. And *being sad* is not identical with *being sad and such that seven and five are twelve*, since, although the latter attribute involves the former, the former does not involve the latter. *Killing* and *being killed* are distinct attributes, since, although they involve each other, they do not *include* each other.

A Mark of the Psychological

We have now defined the terms that occur in our formula:

Any property which is possibly such that it is exemplified by just one thing and which includes every property it implies or involves is psychological.

It is clear that the nonrelational nonpsychological properties we have listed above do not satisfy this formula. Thus the disjunctive property of being either angry or two-legged involves but does not include the property of being angry. One can't *conceive* the disjunctive property without conceiving the property of being angry; but one can *have* the disjunctive property without having the property of being angry. Again, a thing can have the property of being intoxicating without having the property of being intoxicated; but one can't conceive the property of being intoxicating without conceiving the property of being intoxicated. Thus we can say of dispositional properties generally that they involve but do not include the property or properties toward which they dispose their bearers.

But our paradigmatic psychological properties are all such that they include every property that they imply or involve. And, it would seem, only psychological properties satisfy this condition. Hence the formula gives us a *sufficient condition* of the psychological.

Some Test Cases

We now consider certain *nonpsychological* attributes which, at first consideration, may seem to satisfy our formula; that is to say, each of them may seem to be a property which is such that it includes every attribute it implies or involves. But a closer examination will show that these attributes do not satisfy our formula. And in most such cases, we will find that the attribute in question does not satisfy our definition of *property*.

Being a proper part of an individual thing does not satisfy our formula, for it is not possibly such that there is just one thing that has it. So, too, for *having a proper part, being extended*, and *being green*. Anything having any one of these properties has a proper part that also has that property. Therefore these properties are not possibly such that they are exemplified by just one thing.

What of such semantical attributes as *referring to something, designating oneself*, and *being heterological*? These attributes involve but do not include such properties as *using a language* and *interpreting a language*.

What of *moving*? The attribute of moving may be defined as follows: being one of several things that are changing their spatial relations to each other. Hence moving does not satisfy our formula, for it cannot be exemplified by just one individual.

The attribute *undergoing change* is not a property. It is necessarily the case that if anything undergoes change then everything undergoes change. Suppose, for example, that a certain individual thing changes from being red to being green. Then each thing changes in the following way: certain relations it had formerly born just to something red become relations that it now bears to something green. Hence *undergoing change* is capable of being universal. But no property—in our present sense of the term—is capable of being universal.

"What of *changing internally*? If eternal objects change (say, from being such that there are dinosaurs to being such that there are no dinosaurs), this change is only external and is a function of internal changes in individual things. Eternal objects would not change at all if there were no individual things. Therefore the attribute of *changing internally* would seem to be a property that includes every property it implies or involves. But it is not a psychological attribute."

What would be an example of an 'internal change'? I can think only of four types of such change. (i) There are psychological changes — say, the change from being happy to being sad. But these are not counter to our thesis. (ii) Possibly we can say that *coming into being* and *passing away* are internal changes. But, even if we can say this, we cannot say that they are *properties*, for they are not attributes a thing can have at any period of its existence. (iii) There is the attribute of *undergoing rearrangement of parts*. We could say that a material thing changes internally if it has this attribute — i.e., if its proper parts are changing their spatial relations to each other. Thus a watch, if it is running, is undergoing internal change. But this attribute — *having proper parts that are changing their relations to each other* — implies but does not include *being a proper part*. (iv) There is *undergoing a change of causal properties*. But this is not an attribute that can be exemplified by just one individual. For, if an individual undergoes a change of its causal properties, then it is a member of a set of individuals that are changing their relations to each other. Hence this attribute includes the attribute of *being an individual thing which is such that there is an individual discrete from it*. (Two individual things may be said to be *discrete* from each other if they have no parts in common.) But this attribute cannot be exemplified by just one individual. And therefore *undergoing a change of causal attributes* is not a property.

What of *going, functioning, working*? If these are not purely dispositional, or if they are not to be thought of as species of moving, then they imply the property of *being expected to accomplish certain things* or that of *being designed for a certain purpose*. Therefore they involve but do not include the properties of *expecting* or of *designing* or *intending* something.

Useful and *harmful*, if they are not purely dispositional, involve but do not include such properties as *benefiting from something* and *being harmed by something*.

Good and *bad*, if taken as species of intrinsic value, are attributes that are necessary to the things that have them and are therefore not properties. But if they are taken as species of instrumental value, then they are analogous to useful and harmful.

Beautiful and *ugly*, if they are not merely dispositional, involve but do not include such properties as taking pleasure in perceiving something and taking displeasure in perceiving something.

What of *being alive*? It would seem that the word may be taken in two ways. In one sense, 'being alive' connotes a physiological property. And therefore, in this sense, it implies but does not include the property of being a physiological organ. And, in another sense, it is essentially dispositional and thus involves certain properties (physiological or psychological) that it does not imply.

What of *being a person*? It may be plausibly maintained that being a person is necessary to whatever has it and is therefore not a property.

What of *sick* and *healthy*? The words may be taken in one or the other of three different ways—but on no interpretation do they provide us with a counterexample to our thesis. (i) They may refer to certain *physiological* properties; in this case the properties will imply but not include the property of being a physiological organ. (ii) They may be used, psychologically, to mean the same, respectively, as 'feeling ill' and 'feeling well'; in this case, the properties that they connote will satisfy our thesis. Or (iii) the words may be used in a way that is tantamount to a disjunction of the first two uses—to connote the attribute of either being in such and such a physiological state or feeling in such and such a way. In this case, the attribute in question would involve certain attributes it does not include.

We have been unable to find any nonpsychological attribute that satisfies our formula. I conclude, therefore, that the formula gives us a *sufficient condition* of the psychological.

The Definition

We will now propose a definition which will give a *necessary* as well as a sufficient condition of the psychological.

We could say that any attribute satisfying our formula is 'purely qualitative'.

D6 P is a purely qualitative attribute = Df. P is a property which (a) is possibly such that it is exemplified by just one thing and (b) includes every property it implies or involves.

We will now introduce a somewhat broader concept of *qualitative* which will enable us to say that any disjunction of purely qualitative attributes is a qualitative attribute.[1]

D7 P is a qualitative attribute = Df. Either (a) P is a purely qualitative attribute or (b) P is equivalent to a disjunction of attributes each of which is purely qualitative.

Judging and *wanting* will be qualitative by this definition. But *judging that there are unicorns* and *wanting a sloop* will not be qualitative, for each involves a property it does not include. Hence, the above concept is not identical with that of the psychological, since *judging that there are unicorns* and *wanting a sloop* are both psychological attributes.

We can now define a broad sense of the psychological:

D8 P is a psychological attribute = Df. P includes an attribute that is qualitative.

Some attributes that are thus psychological are not *purely* psychological—e.g., believing truly that it is raining and wishing in vain for a sloop. What, then, would a purely psychological attribute be? I suggest this:

D9 P is purely psychological = Df. P is psychological and every property it implies involves something qualitative.

Our definition applies only to those psychological attributes that are nondispositional. But one may wish to say of certain dispositions—being irascible, for example—that they, too, are psychological. Given the concept of a disposition, we could readily extend our definition to such cases. We could say that, in an extended sense of 'psychological attribute', a disposition to have a psychological attribute is itself a psychological attribute.

Concerning those attributes that are purely psychological, we may affirm the following material epistemic principle:

If the attribute of being F is a purely psychological attribute, then, for every x, if x has the attribute of being F, then it is certain for x that he is F.

This principle could be said to tell us that every purely psychological attribute is 'self-presenting'. But the principle does not hold of those attributes that are only 'partly psychological'. A person may have the attribute of thinking while wearing a hat or that of thinking about his brother without thereby being *certain* that he is thinking while wearing a hat or that he is thinking about his brother.[2]

Notes

1. An attribute D may be said to be a *disjunction* of two attributes, P and Q, provided only D involves P and D involves Q, and D is necessarily such that, for every x, x has D if and only if either x has P or x has Q.

2. I am indebted to Fred Feldman, Richard Foley, Richard Potter, Philip Quinn, Allen Renear, Bruno Schuwey, Robert Shope, Ernest Sosa, and Michael Zimmerman.

11

Presence in Absence

An account of intentionality should be adequate to the following two theses: (I) "Mental phenomena can succeed in achieving objective reference" and (II) "Mental phenomena are distinguished by the fact that they may be directed upon objects that do not exist."[1] The second thesis is sometimes said to involve "the problem of error" or "the problem of presence in absence."[2] The first, therefore, might be said to involve "the problem of truth" or "the problem of presence in presence."

Just what are these problems? I will discuss them by reference only to *judging*. But what I will say about judging may also be applied, *mutatis mutandis*, to other intentional attitudes.

The Problem

I will first put the matter somewhat loosely. If a person x judges a thing y to be F, then x makes a judgment which is directed upon y but which is such that one could make that judgment even if y did not exist. For example, if you now judge your neighbor to be a philosopher, then your neighbor may be said to be such that you judge him to be a philosopher. Yet you make a judgment which you could make even if your neighbor didn't exist. How is that possible?

One might say that there is a world which is exactly like what you find this one to be at the time you are judging and which does not contain your neighbor. In such a case, you would be making the judgment you are making now, but your neighbor would not be such that you are making a judgment about *him*. Since, however, your neighbor does exist, your judgment *is* a judgment about him. It is a judgment, with respect to him, that he is a philosopher. And so one asks, "What is there about the judgment, then, that makes it a judgment about *your neighbor*?"[3] The problem is to exhibit the nature of the judging in such a way that we can see both (1) how it is that, your neighbor having the properties he does have, your judging can be said to be *directed upon* him, and also (2) how this same judging could be made even if it were not directed upon anything.

An Attempt at a More Precise Formulation

If a person x judges, with respect to an individual thing y, that y is F, then there is a certain property P which is such that: (1) y has P; and (2) x judges in such a way that (a) necessarily if there is just one thing that has P, then x judges with respect to that thing that it is F and (b) it is possible to judge in that way even if there is not just one thing that has P. We may add (c) that the way of judging is necessarily such that anyone who judges in that way can know directly that he judges in that way.

One way of putting the problem of objective reference, then, would be to ask this: Consider someone x, who judges with respect to something y that it is F; describe x's way of judging so that we may *see* that a judging of that sort is such that (a) it is directed upon something having P, (b) it could be made even if nothing has P, and (c) it is such that anyone who judges in that way can know directly that he judges in that way.

A partial answer would be the following. The judging is of such a nature that, if there happens to be an object having the property P, then the judgment is *directed upon* that object—it is a judgment, *with respect to that object*, that it is F. But unless the object in question is an abstract object, the judging is of such a sort that it could be made even if nothing had the property P. Let us give a name, then, to the relation between the judging and the object that the judging is directed upon. Then we will try to say just what the relation in question is and to explicate what it means to say that a judgment is "directed upon" an object.

Let us say this: "x makes a judgment which *implies that* whatever has P is F." And let us assume, for the moment, that we will be able to specify more exactly the relevant sense of "implies that." Given this much, we could say that x's judgment is *directed upon* a thing y if and only if y is the sole thing having the property P. Then we could answer our philosophical question in the following way.

If you judge your neighbor to be a philosopher and if you have just one neighbor, then you make a judgment which implies him to be a philosopher. The judgment may be said, therefore, to be *directed upon* him. But you *could* make the judgment even if he didn't exist and even if you had no neighbor. For it is possible for it to be the case both (1) that one makes a judgment which implies that whatever has P is F and also (2) that nothing has P. (Strictly speaking, we should specify that P *not* be a property that is essential to some abstract object.)

What is it, then, to make a judgment which *implies that* whatever has P is F? I know of at most four general types of such answer.

The First Type of Theory: Abstract Propositions

The "abstract proposition" theory tells us this:

(1)   x makes a judgment which implies that whatever has P is F = Df x accepts an *abstract proposition* which is necessarily such that (a) it is true if and only if whatever has P is F and (b) whoever conceives it conceives the property of being-F.

If x judges his neighbor to be a philosopher and if y is x's neighbor, then the abstract proposition that x accepts might be one that x could express by saying: "My neighbor is a philosopher."

Why clause (b) in our definition? Without clause (b), the definition would require us to say that whoever judges someone to be a philosopher also judges that person to be such that either he is a philosopher and a Greek or he is a philosopher and a non-Greek. But this consequence would be false.

The theory presupposes, then, that there are abstract objects which are nameable by "that"clauses and sentential gerundives. And it also presupposes that these entities can be grasped or conceived by believing subjects.[4]

If we view intentionality this way, we may say that it is a mistake to suppose that "presence in absence" is the mark of intentionality. For we must distinguish two senses of the expression *"object* of thought." (1) If someone x judges with respect to something y, that it is F, then we may, if we choose, say that y is the "object" of x's thought. In such a case we may go on to say that x could make the judgment he does make even if the judgment had *no* object—in *this* sense of "object." (2) But if we say that the "object" of one's judgment is the abstract proposition that one accepts, then, according to the abstract proposition theory, the judgment is necessarily such that it has an object. It is clear that Brentano uses 'object' in the first way in the following passage: "We can, therefore, define mental phenomena by saying that they are those phenomena which contain an object intentionally within themselves."[5] And it is clear that Russell used the word 'object' in the second sense when, in "Meinong's Theory of Complexes and Assumptions" (1904), he wrote: "every presentation and every belief must have an object other than itself and, except in certain cases where mental existents happen to be concerned, extra-mental."[6]

But the abstract proposition theory has its difficulties. These may be seen if we ask how the theory would deal with those judgments we express by means of demonstratives—such words as 'I', 'you', 'this', and 'that'.[7] One possibility is to interpret the sense of demonstrative expressions by reference to "individual essences" or "haecceities." What abstract proposition would one express in English by saying "I am a musician"? This proposition, according to one suggestion, is like that expressed by saying "The tallest man is a musician," except that where the latter involves the property of being the tallest man, the proposition expressed by saying "I am a musician" involves the speaker's individual essence or haecceity. One might be tempted to argue: "My haecceity is the property of *being me*; it is appropriately called my *individual essence* since it is a property that I have necessarily and that no other thing could possibly have." But *is* there a property expressed by "being me"? How does mine differ from yours? Can we really find a difference? If there are *no* such properties, then, given the abstract proposition theory, how are we to interpret those judgments we express by means of demonstratives?[8]

The Second Type of Theory: Singular Propositions

Instead of appealing to abstract propositions, one may appeal to *concrete*—or *singular*—propositions. Then we would have:

(2)   x makes a judgment which implies that whatever has P is F = DF x accepts a *singular proposition* which is necessarily such that (a) it is true if and only if whatever has P is F and (b) whoever conceives it conceives the property being-F.

The presupposition of this theory is that, if there is an individual thing x which has the property being-F, then there is that singular proposition which is *x-being-F*—an entity which contains x as a "constituent" and which is to be distinguished both from x and from the property being-F.[9] If the wealthiest man is such that you believe him to be generous, then, according to the singular proposition theory, there is a singular proposition, *the wealthiest man being generous*, into which the wealthiest man enters as a constituent and which you accept.

Suppose, then, that there exists an x such that x is the wealthiest man: what of that entity which is *x being generous*? If the wealthiest man *is* generous, then there may be that *fact* or *event* which is his being generous and he could be said to be a "constituent" of that fact or event or to be "directly involved" in it. Singular propositions, however, are not to be identified with facts or events—unless (what seems to me to be very problematic) there are events that do not occur. For the singular proposition theory requires us to say that even if the wealthiest man is *not* generous, there *is* that singular proposition which is *his being generous* and he—the wealthiest man himself—is an actual constituent of it. Surely, we should not feel comfortable about positing such entities.

Moreover, the theory does not appear to be adequate to Castaneda's distinction between what is expressed by (i) "x judges x to be F" and (ii) "x judges *himself* to be F." The second locution implies the first, but not conversely.[10] Suppose that I am looking at a certain photograph which, unsuspected by me, is a photograph of me. I may conclude that the person depicted was a politician without thereby thinking that *I* was a politician. I would be an x such that x judges x to have been a politician, but I would not be an x such that x judges himself to be a politician.

It is clear that, if I am x, there is no distinction between that singular proposition which is *x being a politician* and that singular proposition which is *my being a politician*. It looks, therefore, as though the singular proposition theory requires us to say, incorrectly, that "x judges x to be a politician" and "x judges himself to be a politician" express the same singular proposition.

The Third Type of Theory: Properties

The third type of explication is this:

(3)   x makes a judgment which implies that whatever has P is F = Df x directly attributes to x a *property* which is necessarily such that (a) whatever has it bears a certain relation R just to a thing which has P and to a thing which is F and (b) whoever thus directly attributes that property conceives the relation R.

The property that x directly attributes to himself might be this: having just one neighbor and a neighbor who is a philosopher.

Judging, according to this conception, is fundamentally a matter of *attributing* a property to something. Every judgment includes a *direct* attribution of a property to oneself. I presuppose that one can *directly* attribute properties only to oneself. In other words, direct attribution is necessarily such that, for every x and y, if x directly attributes anything to y, then x is identical with y.

I have defended this conception elsewhere.[11] My present concern is not to define it in detail, but to determine what the alternatives are.

In attributing a property to himself, a person *may* also happen to attribute a property to another thing; in such a case, the person *indirectly* attributes a property to the other thing. If you have just one neighbor and if you directly attribute to yourself the attribute of being a person whose neighbor is a philosopher, then you have indirectly attributed to your neighbor the property of being a philosopher. It is not difficult to find, with respect to *anything* to which we attribute a property, some relation which is such that we bear that relation *only* to the thing to which we attribute the property.

According to this conception, then, the "he, himself" locution comes to this:

x judges himself to be F = DF x directly attributes to x the property of being-F.

Contrast now this locution:

x judges x to be F = Df Either (1) x judges himself to be F; or (2) there is a relation R such that (a) x bears R to y and only to y and (b) x directly attributes to x a property which is necessarily such that (i) whatever has it bears R to something that is F and (ii) whoever conceives it conceives being-F.

Hence we see that, of the two locutions "x judges himself to be F" and "x judges x to be F," the first implies the second and the second does not imply the first.

Is There an "Inner Sentence" Theory?

We may attempt to formulate a fourth type of theory by replacing the reference to "propositions" in our first two formulae by a reference to *sentences*. Then we would have:

(4.1) x makes a judgment which implies that whatever has P is F = DF x accepts a *sentence* which is necessarily such that (a) it is true if and only
if whatever has P is F and (b) whoever conceives it conceives the property being-F.

But this will not do as it stands. The English sentence, "My neighbor is a philosopher" is not *necessarily* such that it is true if and only if my neighbor is a philosopher. For our language could have developed in such a way that "My neighbor
is a philosopher" means something very different.

Perhaps, therefore, one might say something of this sort:

(4.2) x makes a judgment which implies that whatever has P is F = Df S accepts in a language L a *sentence* which in L is necessarily such that (a)
it is true in L if and only if whatever has P is F and (b) whoever understands it in L conceives the property being F.

But what is it "to accept a sentence S in a language L"? One has the feeling
that this comes to no more than: "to accept what it is that S expresses in L." In
this case the inner sentence theory is not an alternative to the other theories.

One may, of course, make a judgment *about* a sentence—a judgment which
is *directed upon* a sentence. And some philosophers would replace "x accepts a
sentence S in L" by something like "x recognizes S in L as expressing his atti-
tude."[12] The latter expression, however, implies "x takes p in L to express his atti-
tude," which, in turn, implies the intentional locution, "x takes y to be F." Hence
this move leaves us with our problem.

It is difficult, therefore, to avoid the conclusion that, despite all that has been
written about the relevance of language to intentionality, there really is *no* linguistic interpretation of intentionality.

These considerations confirm a traditional view that may be expressed by saying "the intentional is prior to the semantical."

Are There Alternatives?

During the past few years there has been an enormous amount of literature
devoted to these problems—much of it containing such expressions as "*noemata*"
and "inner systems of representation." It seems to be thought that there are alternatives which are much more profound than anything suggested by the present
analyses. If there really are such alternatives, one has only to produce formulae
comparable to the four just cited. But I have no idea what the formulae might be.

Notes

    1. Similar theses are formulated by Maurita J. Harney, in *Intentionality, Sense and the Mind*
(The Hague: Martinus Nijhoff, 1984), p. 2.
    2. Josiah Royce discusses "the problem of error" in Chapter 40 ("The Possibility of Error") in
The Religious Aspect of Philosophy (Boston: Houghton Mifflin, 1898), pp. 384–435. William James
uses "presence in absence" in *The Meaning of Truth* (New York: Longmans Green, 1900), p. 44.

James asks what it is for a person to believe that there are tigers in India and observes: "A great mystery is usually made of this peculiar presence in absence; and the scholastic philosophy . . . would explain it as a peculiar kind of existence, called *intentional inexistence*, of the tigers in our mind."

3. Compare Wittgenstein: "What makes my idea of him an idea of *him?*" *Philosophical Investigations* (Oxford: Basil Blackwell, 1953), p. 177. Compare also his *Last Writings on the Philosophy of Psychology*, vol. 1 (Chicago: University of Chicago Press, 1982): "What makes this sentence a sentence that has to do with *him?*" (p. 43).

4. Frege seems to have accepted the abstract proposition theory; see his essay "The Thought: A Logical Inquiry" (1918–19), translated in *Mind*, 65 (1956): 289–311. I believe that Husserl also accepted the abstract proposition theory. At any rate, this is the only way I can interpret what he says about *noemata* in the *Ideen zu einer Phänomenologie und phänomenologischen Philosophie* (Turbingen: Max Niemeyer, 1980), pp. 265–75. Compare Dagfinn Follesdal, "Husserl's Notion of the *Noema*," *Journal of Philosophy*, 66 (1969): 680–87. Russell, in the article referred to below, also seems to accept the abstract proposition theory. The expressions "states of affairs" and "event-types" are sometimes used instead of "abstract propositions" in expressing this theory.

5. *Psychology from an Empirical Standpoint* (London: Routledge & Kegan Paul, 1973), pp. 88–89; *Psychologie vom empirischen Standpunkt*, Zweiter Band, (Hamburg: Felix Meiner Verlag, 1971), pp. 124–25. Brentano seldom used such expressions as "intentional inexistence." In *The Psychology of Aristotle*, he used "exists objectively, i.e., as cognized object within us [*objektiv, d.h. als Erkanntes in uns existiert*]." *Psychology of Aristotle* (Berkeley: University of California Press, 1977), p. 54; compare pp. 77, 210 (n6), and 229 (n23); *Die Psychologie des Aristoteles* (Mainz: Franz Vlircheim, 1867), pp. 80, 120.

6. Bertrand Russell, *Essays in Analysis*, ed. Douglas Lackey (New York: George Brazilier, 1973), p. 21.

7. See John Perry, "Frege on Demonstratives," *Philosophical Review*, 86 (1977): 474–97.

8. Ernest Sosa has suggested that there are two types of proposition—those which are nonperspectival and those which are perspectival; and possibly his distinction may help with some of these difficulties. See Ernest Sosa, "Propositions and Indexical Attitudes," in Herman Paret (ed.), *On Believing: Epistemological and Semiotic Approaches* (Berlin and New York: Walter de Gruyter, 1983), pp 316–32; see esp. pp. 322–23. Compare also his "Consciousness of the Self and of the Present," in James Tomberlin (ed.), *Agent, Language and the Structure of the World* (Indianapolis: Hackett Publishing, 1983), pp. 131–43.

9. Compare David Kaplan, Draft Two of his privately circulated monograph, *An Essay on the Semantics, Logic, Metaphysics and Epistemology of Demonstratives and Other Indexicals* (1977). Kaplan observes that "free variables under an assignment of values are paradigms of what I have been calling *directly referential terms*" (p. 2).

10. See Hector-Neri Castañeda, "He: A Study in the Logic of Self-Consciousness," *Ratio*, 8 (1966): 130–57. Compare also the same author's *Thinking and Doing* (Dordrecht: D. Reidel, 1975), Part I.

11. See *The First Person: An Essay on Reference and Intentionality* (Brighton and Minneapolis: Harvester Press and University of Minnesota Press, 1981); and "The Primacy of the Intentional," *Synthèse*, 61 (1984): 89–108.

12. A recent example is provided by Lynne Rudder Baker, "*De Re* Belief In Action," *Philosophical Review*, 91 (1982): 363–87; see in particular, 380.

12

Questions about Minds

The Mind-Body Problem

What is the mind-body problem? The word "mind" has a number of rather different uses and this fact has led to some confusion in recent discussions. We may distinguish at least five such uses and therefore at least five senses of the "mind-body problem."

(1) We could use the term "mind," as Descartes had used the term "*mens*," to refer to that which has psychological properties — to that which thinks, senses, believes, desires. In this case, we would be using "mind" to mean the same as "person" and hence to designate such entities as you and me. If we use "mind" to mean the same as "person," one form of the mind-body problem would be the question: What is the relation between persons and their bodies? What is the relation, for example, between me and my body? There are two broad possibilities: Either I am identical with my body or I am not identical with it. If I am not identical with my body, then once again there are two possibilities: Either I am identical with something that includes a part of my body or I am not identical with anything that includes a part of my body. In the latter case, what kind of thing am I?

It has been suggested in recent years that "the mind" is related to the body in the way in which the abstract diagram of a computer is related to the computer. But this suggestion cannot be true if "mind" is taken, in the sense just distinguished, to refer to that which *has* psychological properties. For the abstract diagram of a computer is itself a property, an abstract object; but that which has psychological properties — that which senses, thinks, feels, and desires — is an individual thing.

(2) We could also use the term "mind," as many now do, to refer to a person's intellectual capacities. The word is being used in this way when one says, "That person has a good mind," meaning that the person is intelligent. An "investigation

of the mind," in this second sense of the word "mind," would be a psychological investigation of intellectual capacities. In this case, the substantive "mind" may be misleading, since it might be taken to designate an *individual thing* that exists along with the person and his body. In such a case one is mislead into supposing that there are *three* individual things to be related—the person, the person's mind, and the person's body.

Using "mind" in this second way, may we say that there is a mind-body problem? Perhaps there is the question "How can a body have intellectual capacities?" If we may assume that there is *something* that has intellectual capacities, then this version of the mind-body problem reduces to the first: What is the relation between a person and his body? For it is presumably the person who has intellectual capacities.

(3) We may also speak of a person's mind as being *that by means* of which he thinks. In this case the term "mind" *does* designate an individual thing. That by means of which one thinks is quite obviously the brain—or at least something that includes a part of the brain. If we use "mind" in this way (to mean that by means of which one thinks) and not in the first way (to mean the person) and not in the second way (to refer to intellectual capacities), then what we would call an "investigation of the mind" would be a neurophysiological investigation of the brain. And the expression "mind-body problem" would refer to certain questions of neurophysiology. Answers to these neurological questions do not, as such, give us a solution to the "mind-body problem," where this expression is interpreted in accordance with the *first* sense of "mind" distinguished above.

(4) The term "mind" is sometimes used to designate a *spiritual substance*, an individual thing of a nonmaterial nature. (Here, perhaps, the word "soul" is more appropriate.) If, in dealing with the person-body problem, we were to decide that the person is not identical with his body or with anything that includes a part of his body, then we might want to consider the possibility that the person *is* a soul or mind, in the present sense of the word "mind." (If we conclude that the person *is* a soul or mind, then we should take care not to express this conclusion by saying that the person *has* a soul or mind. For then we might be misled, once again, into thinking that we are dealing with *three* types of individual thing—persons, minds, and bodies.)

(5) Finally, "the mind-body problem" is sometimes taken to be that of studying the relation between psychological and physical properties and thereby getting a better understanding, not only of the nature of the psychological, but also that of the physical universe. The concern is with such question as: Is each psychological property *identical* with some physical property? Is each psychological property *dependent* in some special sense upon physical property or upon some set of physical properties? Here, once again, the expression "*mind*-body problem" may be misleading once again; I suggest that "psychophysical problem" would be better.

Most contemporary discussions that purport to be about the mind-body problem are concerned primarily with the psychophysical problem.

Descriptive Psychology

Much of what has been called "philosophy of mind" is concerned with *describing* the psychological states and properties of persons and describing them as they are experienced by those who are in those states or have those properties. One purpose of doing this is to resolve the philosophical perplexity to which some of these states and properties give rise. The hope is thereby better to understand the person who is the subject of such states and properties. This type of philosophy of mind includes, not only the descriptive psychology of Brentano, but also the "phenomenology" of Husserl and the later existentialists, as well as the type of study to be found in Wittgenstein's *Philosophical Investigations*.

Some of the philosophers who have called themselves "phenomenologists" have said that their descriptions are designed to catch the *essences* of such phenomena—the essence, say, of such a phenomenon as being sad. The essence of an *individual thing* would be a set of properties that that thing and only that thing has necessarily and that nothing else could possibly have. Now sadness is a *property* and not an individual thing. Shall we say, then, that the essence of the property sadness is a property of the property sadness—a property that is essential to it and only it and repugnant to every thing else? Then there would be no difficulty in saying what the essence of sadness is: sadness is a property which is necessarily such that it is exemplified in all and only those things that are sad.

When philosophers have said they were describing the essence of sadness, what they may have meant is that they were providing with an *analysis* of sadness. What would that be?

Perhaps this: the philosophers are concerned with a familiar phenomenon and that they are pointing out certain essential properties of it that are revealing but often go unnoticed. If you say, "Sadness is to be analysed as being so-and-so and such-and-such," and if I understand what you are saying, then either I am already acquainted with sadness or I take you to be saying that that which *you* are acquainted with as sadness is so-and-so and such-and-such. In either case, I am able to identify the *analysandum* independently. More generally, if one professes to give an informative statement about the nature of a state or property, then one presupposes that that property can be independently identified. But some philosophers who profess to tell us about the "true nature" of the psychological do not presuppose this.

Such philosophers say that the data to which the descriptive psychologists appeal are themselves doubtful, being comparable to the old wives' tales of "folk psychology." These philosophers are apparently concerned with what psychological states and psychological properties would be if (1) psychology were a science in the sense in which physics and chemistry may be said to be science and if, nevertheless, (2) psychology were to investigate psychological states and properties. The concern, then, is with such questions as "What sorts of things might appropriately be called 'believing,' 'feeling,' 'sensing,' and the like if psychology were a natural science?" Sometimes it is suggested that what might then be called "psychological" or "mental" would be very different from the psychological states and properties that we are in fact acquainted with. In this case, the philosophers may have no theory about the nature of those psychological properties that *we* are directly acquainted with, since they may profess not to believe that there are such properties. It is difficult, therefore, to evaluate their statements since it is not clear what they take as their data or what they would accept as confirmation or as falsification of what they are trying to say.

The Psychophysical Problem

The authors of the *Wissenschaftliche Weltauffassung* and those who followed them in the tradition of "physicalism" hoped to be able to identify psychological states and properties with physical states and properties. But with *what* physical states and properties? The program seemed promising in the case of sensations where, it was thought, there is a physical correlate that is unique to every type of sensation. One could then propose as a general hypothesis that each sensation is identical with its physical correlate. But there was difficulty finding such correlates for intentional phenomena (e.g., believing, hoping, questioning, desiring). With what physical state, for example, are we to identify the desire to own a 23-foot sloop? There would seem to be no identifiable physical state that is uniquely correlated with such a desire.

It came to be thought, therefore, that such intentional phenomena might be identified, not with physical *states* or *properties*, but with *dispositions to behave*. A crude form of this view would be that you desire to own a 23-foot sloop if and only if you would respond affirmatively when asked whether you desire to own a 23-foot sloop. But this biconditional needs to be qualified. Thus it could be false if you do *not* desire such a sloop but wish to deceive someone into thinking that you do. And it could be false if you *do* desire such a sloop but do not understand the language of the one who is questioning you. Can we find suitable qualifications, then, to add to the biconditional? The difficulty is that the qualifications we must add to deal with such examples will refer to *other* intentional phenomena — for example, to other things that you desire or do not desire, to what you believe or do not believe, to what you perceive, and to what you remember. Such a theory could hardly be said to reduce psychological phenomena to dispositions to behave — since the relevant dispositions can be described only by reference to other psychological phenomena.

Could one defend a psychophysical identity thesis without appeal to a psychophysical *correlation* thesis? One cannot say, of course, that a thing may be identical with one thing at one time and with *another* thing at another time. But it has been suggested that the *particular occurrences* ("tokens") of any given psychological property may be such that some are identical with the particular occurrences of one physical property and others are identical with the particular occurrences of some other physical property. But what ground is there for the metaphysical thesis according to which there *are* such particular occurrences (tokens) of properties? So far as I have been able to see, the thesis has no basis at all — other than the possibility that it might help us with the psychophysical problem. The metaphysical price of accepting this metaphysical doctrine in order to preserve the psychophysical identity theory seems very high, especially when we consider that this "token-token" version of the theory is *par excellence*, a theory which is neither verifiable nor falsifiable.

Some "functionalists" have said, in effect, that even though a piecemeal reduction of the psychological to the physical is not possible, a wholesale reduction is possible. The point is, not to identify particular psychological states (such as desiring a 23-foot sloop) with neurological states or with dispositions to behave in certain particular ways, but to identify one's *total* psychological state at any time one's total physical state at that time. Such a theory is no longer in the spirit of the *Wissenschaftliche Weltauffassung*, for, like the "token-token" theory just considered, it would seem to be a paradigm case of a theory that is neither verifiable nor falsifiable.

13

Is There a Mind-Body Problem?

The title—"Is there a Mind-Body Problem?"—will suggest that I have doubts as to whether there is a mind-body problem. And I do have doubts as to whether there is a special problem concerning the relation between *the mind* and the body. You may say: "Well, plenty of people have worried about the problem of the relation of the mind and the body. And so therefore there is a problem." And of course that is true enough: people have been concerned with it. But what I wish to suggest is that they shouldn't have been concerned with it: there is no evidence to suggest that I have something to be called *a mind* which we must relate somehow to the body.

Now in saying this—there is no reason to suggest that I have something to be called a mind—I do not mean to say that there is no *person*-body problem. If we use "person" to designate such entities as you and me, then there is no question but that there *are* such things as persons. And obviously there is no question but that there *are* such things as our bodies. There *is* a problem about the relation between *those* entities. Thus there is the question: What is the relation between me and my body? There are two broad possibilities: Either I am identical with my body or I am not identical with it. And if we decide that I am not identical with it, then once again there are two possibilities: Either I am identical with some part of my body or I'm not. And If I'm not, then just what kind of thing am I? So there is a person-body problem.

But I want to urge that we multiply problems beyond necessity if we suppose, that in *addition* to the person-body problem, there is *also* a mind-body problem. In suggesting that there is *no* mind-body problem, then, I am suggesting this: if the substantival expression "mind" is taken to designate some individual thing which is *other* than the person, something that person may be said to *have*, just as it has a hand and a foot, then there is no reason to suppose that there is such a thing as the mind; and if there is no reason to suppose that there is such a thing as the mind, then there is no problem about how it may be related to the body.

One Case for Minds

So let us ask, then, "Why assume that there is such a thing as my mind?" This is different from asking "Why assume that there is such a thing as me?" And it is also different from asking "Why assume that I have various *mental* properties and potentialities, such as the the ability to think or to think in such ways?" For the assumption that *I* have these mental properties and potentialities doesn't imply that I have a mind which has them.

Why should one suppose that there is a nonmaterial thing which is the mind?

Aristotle had argued that "that in the soul which is called mind (by mind I mean that whereby the soul thinks and judges) . . . cannot reasonably be regarded as blended with body."[1] The mind, he said, must be "capable of receiving the form of an object" but without thereby becoming that object.[2] And this would be impossible if the mind were itself a material thing.

Aristotle's reasoning was essentially this: (1) If you apprehend a thing—say, a dog—then you do it by means of something which bears a certain intimate relation to the form or nature of a dog. But (2) a material thing couldn't bear the requisite relation to the form or nature of a dog unless the material thing were thereby to become itself a dog. On the other hand (3) a nonmaterial thing could bear the requisite relation *without* thereby becoming a dog. Hence if you and I can apprehend dogs, and of course we can, then it is by means of a certain *nonmaterial* thing which is our mind.

What are we to say of this argument? The argument requires a more specific characterization of the relation in question—the relation that must be born to the form or nature of a dog if one is to be able to apprehend a dog. Until we have such an account, I think we must say that both premise (1) and premise (2) are problematic.[3]

Perhaps the most important consideration which may make us wonder whether there is a nonmaterial substance which is a mind is the nature of our immediate experience—our experience of what are sometimes called "sense-data" or "appearances." Let us consider one twentieth-century conception of appearances, for this was thought by many to demonstrate an irreducible dualism between mind and body. I am referring to the view set forth by A. O. Lovejoy in his book *The Revolt Against Dualism* (1930).

"No man doubts," Lovejoy wrote, "that when he brings to mind the look of a dog he owned when a boy, there is something of a canine sort immediately present to and therefore compresent with his consciousness, but that it is quite certainly not that dog in the flesh" (p. 305). The thing that is there—the something of a canine sort that is immediately before the mind—is not itself a physical object, Lovejoy said; it is a private, psychological object, conditioned by a series of physiological and psychological events, reaching back to the earlier dog which it now reveals.

If the man now looks at his desk, then, according to Lovejoy, there is another series of physiological and psychological events, this time involving the activity of sense organs, but resulting as before in a private, psychological object—a sensation, this time something of a desk sort, a "visible desk" which in certain respects serves to duplicate the real, external, physical desk which it makes known to us.

Both of these examples—the earlier dog and the external desk being presented by an inner visual desk—provide us with the essentials of two philosophical theories, which Lovejoy had referred to as "epistemological dualism" and "psychophysical dualism." According to "epistemological dualism," which is a thesis about our knowledge, we have direct or imemdiate knowledge only of certain private or subjective states; some external objects, past or present, are "duplicated" in these private or subjective states and it is in virtue of this duplication that we know what we do about the rest of the world. Our knowledge of external things and of past events involves a "cleavage" between the *object* of our knowing and the subjective *vehicle* which makes that object known. And according to "psychophysical dualism," which is a thesis about reality, the world is constituted out of at least two fundamentally different kinds of stuff—the physical or material things that are studied by physics, and the psychical or mental things that are objects of our private or subjective states. When asserted in conjunction, as they were by Lovejoy, and in the seventeenth century by Descartes and Locke, these two forms of dualism imply that our knowledge of physical or material things is derived from our knowledge of the mental or psychical duplicates of these things.

Our present interest is in the second of these types of dualism—psychophysical dualism, the view that there is a set of mental or psychical entities, which are appearances or sense-data, and that these psychical entities are housed in a psychical place, known as "the mind."

The Sense-Datum Fallacy

Let us begin by considering those strange entities which are sense-data or appearances.

It was supposed, for example, that if a man were to walk around a table, while focusing on the white tablecloth on the top, he could experience a great variety of sense-data or appearances. Some of these entities would be rectangular like the tabletop itself; they would be the ones he would sense if he were to get his head directly above the table and then look down. Most of them, however, would be rhomboids of various sorts. If the lighting conditions were good and the man's eyes in proper order, most of the appearances would be white, like the tablecloth. But if the man were wearing rose-colored glasses, he might sense appearances that were pink, or if he were a victim of jaundice, he might sense appearances that were yellow. The other senses, as well as imagination, were thought to bring us into relation with still other types of appearances or sense-datum.

It was assumed that, if a physical thing appears white or rhomboidal or bitter to a man, then the man may be said to sense or to be aware of an appearance that *is* white, or an appearance that *is* rhomboidal, or an appearance that *is* bitter. It was assumed that if a dog presents a canine appearance, then the dog presents an appearance that *is* canine.[4] And it was assumed, more generally, that whenever we have a true statement of the form "Such-and-such a physical thing appears, or looks, or seems so-and-so to Mr. Jones," we can derive a true statement of the form "Mr. Jones is aware of an appearance which is in fact so-and-so." But this assumption is quite obviously false.[5]

Consider the following reasoning, which would be quite sound if the assumption were true: "That dog looks vicious and more than 10 years old. Therefore he presents an appearance which *is* vicious and he presents an appearance which *is* more than 10 years old." It is absurd to suppose that an appearance, like a dog or a man, may be vicious or more than 10 years old. It is also absurd to suppose that an appearance may be a *dog* — i.e., something of a "canine sort." And, I think, it is equally absurd to suppose that an appearance, like a tablecloth, may be rectangular, or pink, or white.

We should compare the grammer of (a) "I sense a red appearance," (b) "I have a depressed feeling," and (c) "I have a green Chevrolet." The sense-datum philosopher interprets (a) as though it resembled (c) more than (b). But I suggest that it should be taken in such a way that it resembles (b) more than (c). Thus "I have a depressed feeling" should not be taken to say that I have a feeling that is itself depressed. It doesn't predicate *being depressed* of a feeling; it predicates *feeling depressed* of a person. And "I sense a canine appearance" doesn't predicate caninity of an appearance. It predicates being appeared to in-a-certain-way to me. I'm appeared to in a way that is optimal for the perception of dogs. Being appeared to is an undergoing — a nonrelational quality of the person.

And so, if what we have said is correct, then *one* of Lovejoy's arguments for *psychophysical dualism* — the dualism of mind and body — is inconclusive. For Lovejoy had argued: (1) We see desks and stars and other objects by means of internal desks and stars which are not identical with the objects they enable us to perceive; but (2) no place among physical objects can be found for such internal desks and stars; therefore (3) the latter objects inhabit "the world of the mind" and not "the world of matter." But if premise (1) is false, *this* argument for psychophysical dualism is no longer available. Since there *are* no internal desks and stars, the materialists need not be asked to find a place for them. (But he must, of course, fit the fact of *appearing* into his scheme of things.)

But does this settle the matter? What if being sad and being appeared red to are undergoings — and not relations between persons and sense-data? Isn't there something special about these undergoings? After all, they seem to give the world a "qualitative dimension" it might otherwise not have.[6] And isn't this qualitative dimension a mental or psychical aspect of the world?

Let us try to do justice to this. In particular, let us consider what has sometimes been called the "double aspect" theory. I think that those who spoke this way may have been on the right track.

The Daylight View of Matter

The property of *being depressed*, I have said, is not a property of a feeling and the property of *being red* is not a property of a sense-datum. But *feeling depressed* and *being appeared to redly* are properties of the person—they are nonrelational qualities of the person. So, too, for those other properties that present us with "a qualitative dimension of being." They are all "modifications" of the subject of experience.

But if the subject of experience thus exhibits a "qualitative dimension of being," then doesn't the subject have certain *mental* properties thereby? And doesn't this mean that the subject—the person—is a *mind*?

It may be natural to say that such a qualitative dimension is "mental," and this statement is harmless enough if "mental" is taken to mean the same as "that which is known immediately." For being appeared to *is* mental in that respect: roughly speaking, it can't happen to you unless you know that it is happening to you. But this use of the adjective "mental" should not be taken to suggest the substantive "mind." There is no reason to suppose that only minds can have mental properties in this sense of the word "mental." It is possible that, in this sense of "mental," physical things may have properties that are "mental." Or to put the matter more carefully, it is possible that there are things having properties that are physical and also having properties that are mental.

These remarks will recall what has sometimes been called "the double aspect theory." The theory may be put by saying that persons have "inner" and "outer" aspects. The "inner" aspects are "mental"; that is to say, they are those subjective and intentional properties which are necessarily such that, if a person has them, then it is evident to the person that he has them. And the "outer" aspects are certain physical properties.

It is essential not to confuse this use of the expression "double aspect" with certain other uses that the expression has been given in recent philosophy. Thus we are using it for the view according to which certain *individual things*—namely persons—have both "mental" and "physical" properties. But it has also been used for the view according to which there are certain *events* or *activities* having both mental and physical properties.[7] The latter view is quite different from the one that I have suggested. (Obviously, it would be a category mistake of the most egregious kind to identify persons with events or activities.) The expression "double aspect" theory has also been used for the so-called identity-theory, according to which "mental events" are to be identified with "physical events."[8] But "the double aspect theory," as I use this term, refers to a theory about the nature of persons and not to a theory about events.

The double aspect view has been clearly set forth by Gustav Theodor Fechner.[9] Thus he held that we are "to ourselves" psychical and "to others" material. The important point of his doctrine, it seems to me, is the assertion that we are *both* mental and material. For the assertion implies that what is material can also be mental. A material thing can be "intrinsically psychical."

Perhaps we could accept this conclusion without holding, as Fechner did, that *all* matter is intrinsically psychical. But if *some* material things are intrinsically psychical, what about the others? What could *their* intrinsic properties be? Do we know of any intrinsic properties other than those we have been calling psychical? Or is it possible that only some individual things *have* intrinsic properties and hence that others have *no* intrinsic properties?

The word "intrinsic" has two senses here. One is suggested by the concept of "self-presentation"; Fechner says that certain things are "psychical to themselves," and this means that they have certain states that "present themselves." The other sense of "intrinsic" is that of nonrelational: an intrinsic property of a thing would be a property not entailing relations of the thing to other things.

Fechner called this the "daylight view" (*die Tagesansicht*) of matter and contrasted it with the "night view" of matter.[10]

The "double aspect theory" tells us this: There are certain things which have physical properties and therefore physical objects; some of these things also have certain mental or intentional properties; and persons — you and I — are such things as these.

C.A. Strong put this last point clearly. He wrote:

> *I* am to outer appearance physical but to inner perception psychical; there is therefore no contradiction in a thing being at once physical, that is, extended, composed of parts, productive of effects, and psychical, that is of the nature of feeling.[11]

Strong is not here saying that "my mind" is an aspect of a physical thing, much less that *I* am an aspect of a physical thing. What he says is that there *is* a certain physical thing which has inner and outer aspects and that that physical thing is identical with me.

"Which Physical Thing Am I?"

If we were to accept this theory, then we could ask: "*Which* physical thing am I?" I am afraid we could not provide a precise answer to this question.

If I am in fact a physical thing, then, it should be obvious, that physical thing is either this gross physical body now standing before you or it is some proper part of this gross physical body. There are, of course, many philosophical arguments professing to show that the person cannot be identical with his gross macroscopic physical body. Some of these arguments, I think, are sound — in particular those appealing to certain facts about persistence through time.

The body that persists through time — the one I have been carrying with me, so to speak — is an *ens successivum*. That is to say, it is an entity made up of different things at different times. The set of things that make it up today is not identical with the set of things that made it up yesterday or with the set of things that made it up the day before. Now one could say that an *ens successivum* has different "stand-ins" at different times and that these stand-ins do duty for the successive entity at the different times. Thus the thing that does duty for my body today is other than the thing that did duty for it yesterday and other than the thing that will do duty for it tomorrow. But what of me?

Am *I* an entity such that different things do duty for *me* at different days? Is it *one* thing that does my feeling depressed for me today and *another* thing that did it yesterday and still another thing that will do it tomorrow? If I happen to be feeling sad, then, surely, there is no *other* thing that is doing my feeling sad for me. We must reject the view that persons are thus *entia successiva*.

Our reasoning can be summarized. Suppose (i) that I am now sad. Now (ii) if there is an *ens successivum* that bears my name and is now sad, then it is sad in virtue of the fact that one of its stand-ins is now sad. But (iii) I am not sad in virtue of the fact that some *other* thing is doing my feeling sad for me. Therefore (iv) I am not an *ens successivum*.

What would be an *ens nonsuccessivum*? If an individual thing were a nonsuccessive entity, what would it be like? If an *ens successivum* is an individual thing that is made up of different things at different times, then an *ens nonsuccessivum* would be an individual thing that is *not* made up of different things at different times. This means that, at any moment of its existence, it has precisely the same parts it has at any other moment of its existence; at no time during which it exists, does it have a part it does not have at any other time during which it exists.

It is tempting to reason, in Leibnizian fashion: "There are *entia successiva*. Therefore there are *entia nonsuccessiva*." I believe this reasoning is sound. I would add, moreover, that every extended period of time, however short, is such that some *ens nonsuccessivum* exists during some part of that time. For I believe it is only by presupposing this thesis that we can make sense of the identity or persistence of *any* individual thing through time.

Might I not be, then, such an *ens nonsuccessivum*? Leibniz mentions—and rejects—a theory which is similar to this. "The soul," he says, "does not dwell in certain atoms appropriated to itself, nor in a little incorruptible bone such as the *Luz* of the Rabbis."[12] Of course, the hypothesis I have suggested, if filled in by reference to such a material thing as the *Luz* bone, would not imply that "the soul" dwells there—if the soul is understood to be something *other* than the person, still another thing that the person "has." We would be saying rather that the person dwells there. And to say that he "dwells" there would be to say that the person *is* the *Luz* bone or some proper part of it.

If we accept this theory, then, of course, we part company with personalism. The doctrine that persons are physical things—even intactly persisting physical things—would not have been taken seriously by Borden Parker Bowne and his followers. Yet, if we view the person in the way I have suggested, we may go on to affirm many of the *other* philosophical theses that the personalists felt to be important. Thus we could say, as Bishop Butler did, that "our gross organized bodies with which we perceive the objects of sense, and with which we act, are no part of ourselves. . . . We see with our eyes in the same way we see with our glasses."[13] The eyes are the *organs* of sight, not the *subject* of sight. We could say, as Butler and the personalists did, that the destruction of the gross physical body does not logically imply the destruction of the person. And we could accept the view that St. Thomas attributes to Plato: the person is "in a body in somewhat the same way as a sailor is in a ship."[14]

Some Objections Considered

To understand the view that is being proposed, let us formulate certain objections that readily come to mind and then attempt to reply to them. I will consider four such objections.

(1) "The hypothesis you are considering implies, then, that there is a kind of matter that is incorruptible and that the person is a material thing of that sort? But this is hardly adequate to the facts of physics."

The reply is that the theory does not imply that there is certain matter that is incorruptible. It implies rather that there are certain material things—in all probability, certain material particles or subparticles—that are incorrupted and remain incorrupted as long as the person survives.

The theory would be, then, that I am literally identical with some proper part of this macroscopic body, some intact, nonsuccessive part that has been in this larger body all along. This part is hardly likely to be the *Luz* bone, of course; more likely, it would be something of a microscopic nature, and presumably something that is located within the brain.

(2) "Persons, being thinking things, must have a complex structure. But no microscopic entity that is known to physics has the equipment that is necessary for thinking. After all, you can't think unless you have a brain. And *those* little things don't have brains!"

The hypothesis being criticized is the hypothesis that *I* am such a microscopic entity. But note that I do have a brain. And therefore, according to the hypothesis in question, the microscopic entity has one, too—the same one that I have, the one that is inside my head. It is only a confusion to suppose that the microscopic entity—which may in fact be inside my brain—has *another* brain which is in fact inside of it.[15]

The brain is the *organ* of consciousness, not the *subject* of consciousness— unless I am myself my brain.[16] The nose, similarly, is the organ of smell and not the subject of smell—unless I am myself my nose. But if I am one or the other— the brain or the nose—then, I the subject, will have some organs that are spatially outside me.

The hypothesis in question, then, is that I am a certain proper part of my brain. This would imply that the subject of consciousness is a proper part of the organ of consciousness.

(3) "You say I'm identical with some microscopic particle or some subparticle. But I am 6 feet tall and weigh 175 pounds. Therefore your theory would imply that there is a certain microscopic particle which is 6 feet tall and weighs 175 pounds. But this is absurd and therefore your theory is absurd."

The argument, of course, errs in taking too literally the premise expressed by saying "I am 6 feet tall and weigh 175 pounds." For what the premise actually tells us is that I have a body which is 6 feet tall and weighs 175 pounds.

(4) "Do you mean to suggest seriously, then, that instead of weighing 175 pounds, you may weigh less than a milligram?" The answer has to be yes. We must be ready, therefore, to be ridiculed, for, in this case, even those who know better may be unable to resist the temptation. But those who do know better will realize that a person can truly say, in *one* sense, that he weighs 175 pounds, and in *another* sense, that he weighs less than a milligram. The formulation of the first statement would be more nearly accurate (I say "more nearly *accurate*," not "more nearly correct") if it read: "I have a body that weighs 175 pounds."

Speaking in a loose and popular sense, I may attribute to myself certain properties of my gross macroscopic body. (And speaking to a filling station attendant I may attribute certain properties of my automobile to myself: "I'm down there on the corner of Jay Street without any gasoline." The response needn't be: "How, then, can you be standing here?" One might say that the property of being down there is one I have "borrowed" from my automobile.) But if I am a microscopic part of my gross body, then, strictly and philosophically, one cannot attribute to *me* the properties of *it*. The properties of weighing 175 pounds and being 6 feet tall are properties I "borrow" from my body. Strictly and philosophically, *it* has them and I do not.[17]

Conclusion

What are the possibilities, after all? There *are* persons. Therefore either the person is a physical thing or, as Lovejoy suggests, the person is a nonphysical thing. But does anything we know about persons justify us in assuming that persons are *nonphysical* individual things?

If I am a physical thing, then the most plausible hypothesis would seem to be that I am a proper part of this gross microscopic body, even if there is no way / a of telling from the "outside" which proper part I happen to be.

If I am a nonphysical thing, then either I am composed of some nonphysical stuff or I am a monad. But what kind of "stuff" could be nonphysical?

Notes

1. *De Anima*, 429a.

2. Ibid.

3. "In the picture and the pictured there must be something identical in order that the one can be a picture of the other at all." L. Wittgenstein, *Tractatus Logico-Philosophicus*, 2.161.

4. A. O. Lovejoy, *The Revolt Against Dualism* (La Salle, Ill.: Open Court, 1930), p. 305.

5. "The general rule which one may derive from these examples is that the propositions we ordinarily express by saying that a person *A* is perceiving a material thing *M*, which appears to him to have the quality *x*, may be expressed in the sense-datum terminology by saying that *A* is sensing a sense-datum *s*, which really has the quality of *x*, and which belongs to *M*." A. J. Ayer, *The Foundations of Empirical Knowledge* (New York: MacMillan, 1940), p. 58.

6. This expression is used by Roy Wood Sellars, in *Evolutionary Naturalism* (Chicago: University of Chicago Press, 1922), pp. 306–7.

7. For example, by R. J. Hirst, *The Problems of Perception* (London: Allen & Unwin, 1959), p. 189.

. 8. Compare Herbert Feigl, "Physicalism, Unity of Science and the Foundations of Psychology," in P. A. Schilpp (ed.), *The Philosophy of Rudolf Carnap* (La Salle, Ill., Open Court, 1963), pp. 227–267; see p. 254.

9. See in particular his *Uber die Physikaalische und die Philosophische Atomlehre* (1855) and *The Little Book of Life After Death* (English translation, 1912).

10. *Die Tagesansicht Gegenueber der Nachtansicht*, 1879.

11. C. A. Strong, "Final Observations," *Journal of Philosophy*, 38 (1941): 233–43; the quotation is on p. 237.

12. *New Essays Concerning Human Understanding*, Book II, Chap. 28 (La Salle, Ill., Open Court, 1916). p. 242. Alfred Langley, editor of this edition of Leibniz, quotes an ancient discussion of the *Luz* bone: "The old Rabbis of blessed memory have not only seen this bone, but have found it actually so strong and hard that their hammer and rock flew in pieces before this bone was injured in the least" (p. 242n).

13. Joseph Butler, *The Analogy of Religion*, Part I, Chap. 1 ("Of a Future Life"); See *The Whole Works of Joseph Butler. LL.D.* (London: Thomas Tegg, 1839), p. 7.

14. St. Thomas Aquinas, *On Spiritual Creatures*: Article II (Milwaukee: Marquette University Press, 1949), p. 35.

15. I have illustrated this confusion in Richard Taylor's *Action and Purpose* (Englewood Cliffs, N.J., Prentice-Hall, 1966), p. 137.

16. Compare Franz Brentano, *Religion Und Philosophie* (Bern: A. Francke Verlag, 1954).

17. Strawson emphasizes that persons have both psychological and physical properties. But, if what I say is true, most of the physical properties that we ordinarily attribute to the person are "borrowed" in this sense from the person's body.

14

The Primacy of the Intentional

According to the thesis of the primacy of the intentional, the reference of language is to be explicated in terms of the intentionality of *thought*. The word *"Pferd,"* for example, refers to horses insofar as it is used to express thoughts that are directed on horses. But most contemporary philosophers of language, until recently at least, have held that the intentionality of thought is to be explicated in terms of the reference of *language*. But no such explication is at hand.

I will suggest what one can say about the reference of language if one presupposes the primacy of the intentional. I will not use any undefined semantical concepts, since all such concepts, I believe, can be explicated only by reference to intentional concepts. Therefore, I will not speak of "inner systems of representation," "inner speech acts," or "inner language." But I will make use of a number of *intentional* concepts. In terms of these and certain other familiar concepts, I will formulate intentional definitions of such semantic concepts as *sense* and *reference*. I will try to show how this approach will throw light upon a number of philosophical questions (e.g., "How are we to interpret the 'he, himself' locution?" and "Do demonstratives and proper names have senses?").

Language Intentionally Considered

Two assumptions underlie what might be called the orthodox approach to the analysis of sense and reference. One of these is ontological and the other is psychological. Each seems to me questionable.

(1) The first assumption is this: For each use of any well-formed indicative sentence in our language, there is a *proposition* which is the meaning of that sentence in that use.

I would say that this is not an assumption with which we should *begin* our investigations. It is, at best, a conclusion we might draw at the *end* of our investigations. For the "propositions" that are thus presupposed will not be restricted to the abstract objects now commonly called "states of affairs." Those "singular propositions" that would constitute the meanings of sentences containing demonstratives and proper names would be contingent things, dependent for their being on those individual things that are thought to "enter into them." And these singular propositions are strange entities.

There *is* a certain plausibility in the assumption that there are what might be called "concrete *states* or *events*." It is reasonable to assume, after all, that if a contingent thing x has a certain property P, then there is also that concrete state or event that is *x having P*. But concrete states or events will not do the work that is required of singular propositions. For *false* or *nonoccurent* singular propositions would be needed to constitute the meanings of sentences that are false. If you believe that there are 12 planets, then, even if there are only 9 planets, the singular proposition theory requires the existence of that contingent thing which is *there being 12 planets* (or *that there are 12 planets*).

(2) Since, presumably, we can believe only what we can *grasp*, or *conceive*, the singular proposition theory presupposes further that the believer is able to grasp or conceive not only those abstract objects which are properties and states of affairs, but also those contingent "singular propositions" constituting the meanings of sentences containing demonstratives and proper names. It is presupposed that demonstrative terms and proper names, like such definite descriptions as "the tallest spy," have what might be called a *Fregean sense*. A Fregean sense is a property that is such that a term having that sense designates a thing only if the thing has that property. One then looks in vain for those properties constituting the Fregean senses of demonstratives ("this," "I," "you," "now") and of proper names ("Tom," "Cicero").

The conception of intentionality that I shall set forth is considerably simpler than the foregoing and it has a number of advantages as a basis for understanding language.

De Re Belief

I will assume that intentional attitudes involve a relation between a person and a *property* or *attribute* rather than between a person and a *proposition*. I shall set forth this view in some detail in application to occurrent belief—or *believing*—and somewhat more sketchily in connection with *endeavoring* and *perceiving*. What is said about these attitudes may also be applied, *mutatis mutandis*, to *thinking*, or *considering*.[1]

We begin, then, with *believing*.

I presuppose that believing is essentially a matter of believing certain properties *"directly of oneself."* (We could also say: "attributing certain properties directly to oneself.") The fundamental doxastic concept may be expressed by the locution *x believes directly of y the property of being-F*

a locution that is taken to imply

x is identical with y

The letter "F" in "being-F" is schematic and may be replaced by any English predicate — say, "wise." The result of such replacement will be the English *term* "being-wise" — a term designating a property.

What would it be, then, for one to have a belief about something *other* than oneself? Suppose, for example, that I believe *you* to be wise. In this case, there is a property I believe directly of me; this property relates me just to you; and because of this relation, I can be said to believe being-wise *indirectly* of you. Such a belief might come about under the following circumstances. You are the person I am talking with; and the property of talking with just one person and with a person who is wise is a property that I attribute directly to myself.

We may be tempted, then, to characterize indirect attribution this way:

x believes being-F indirectly of y = Df There is a relation R such that (a) x bears R only to y and (b) the property of bearing R to just one thing and to a thing that is F is one that x believes directly of x

Then we could say that *x believes y to be F* provided only that x believes being-F either directly or indirectly of y. But this preliminary account may be more latitudinarian than it should be.

Consider the following example, adapted from one suggested by Keith Donnellan.[2]

(1) I believe that the person I am looking at is a member of the Temperance Union; (2) I believe, mistakenly, that the person I am looking at is the only one at the party who is drinking a martini; (3) putting two and two together, I judge that the only one at the party who is drinking a martini is a member of the Temperance Union; and (4) as it happens, the only one at the party who is drinking a martini is not the person I am looking at, but the person who is standing behind me.

Application of our formula above to this example would require us to say not only that the person I'm looking at, but also that the person who is standing behind me, is such that I believe that *he* is a member of the Temperance Union. My belief, so to speak, "points to" both individuals. But if it is a belief that is *directed on* one of them, then it is not also a belief that is directed on the other.

If my belief is directed on a specific individual, say, *you*, then I have some conception of just *who* you are. But in what sense of "conceiving who you are"?

First I will put the answer somewhat loosely. Then I will attempt a more precise formulation.

If my belief is directed on you, then there are two things to be said about the *justification* that I have for that belief: (1) the property by means of which I relate myself uniquely to you is one such that I am justified in believing that there is just one thing having it; and (2) at the moment I have no *better* way of identifying you.

In putting the account of indirect attribution more exactly, I will use "x believes himself to be F" as short for "the property of being F is such that x believes it directly of x":

D1 x believes indirectly with respect to y that it is F = DF There is a relation R such that:
    (1) x bears R just to y;
    (2) x judges himself to bear R to just one thing and to a thing that is F;
    (3) x is more justified in judging himself to bear R to just one thing than in not judging himself to bear to just one thing; and
    (4) if x judges himself to bear R to the thing he bears S to, then he is at least as justified in judging himself to bear R to just one thing as he is in judging himself to bear S to just one thing

If, in judging that he is talking with a member of the Temperance Union, x has a belief that is directed upon y, then: (1) x is more justified in believing that there is one and only person he is talking with than in having such a belief; and (2) if x also judges that the person he is talking with is, say, *the Chairman* of the Temperance Union, then he, x, is at least as justified in believing that there is just one person he is talking with as in believing that there is just one person who is the Chairman of the Temperance Union.

And now we may set forth our definition of *de re* belief:

D2 x believes with respect to y that it is F = Df The property of being F is such that x believs it either directly or indirectly of y

On this account, the *de dicto* locution, "x accepts the proposition that p" could be defined as: "There is a y such that x believes with respect to it that it is true."

We should note, in passing, that this epistemic conception of *de re* belief may also be adapted to the propositional conception of intentionality. One could say:

x believes with respect to y that it is F =DF
    (1) x believes that the G is F;
    (2) y is the G;
    (3) x is more justified in believing that there is just one thing that is G than in not believing that there is just one thing that is G; and
    (4) if x believes that the G is the H, then x is at least as justified in believing that there is just one thing that is G as he is in believing that there is just one thing that is H

Object and Content

The distinction between *object* and *content* is essential to understanding language. In saying something to you, my concern may be to get you to *believe* something. Or it may be to get you to *do* something. Or it may be merely to get you to *think* of something. In each case, there is a distinction between object and content. Thus there is the object, or there are the objects, that I want you to believe something *about*, or to do something *to*, or to think of in a certain *way*. And there is what it is that I want you to believe about the object, or what it is I want you to do to the object, or what it is I want you to think of the object as being.

Suppose you are driving a car in which I am a passenger and I say to you urgently: "That green Chevrolet over there is out of control!" If you reply, "That's not a Chevrolet," you may correct what I say, but you will have misinterpreted my message. I might reply, if there is time, "But whatever it is it's out of control!"[3] The words "That green Chevrolet is out of control" in my original utterance did not express any part of the *content* I meant to convey. I used them only so that you would pick out the *object* I want to convey something about. The *content* of my message was expressed by the words "out of control."

Since, in believing, one directly attributes a property to oneself and in so doing one may indirectly attribute another property to some other thing, we may distinguish between the *direct* and the *indirect* object and content of belief. And analogously for the other intentional attitudes. Thus, we may distinguish between the object and the content of *thinking of* and between the object and content of *endeavor*.

Perceiving and Endeavoring

The concept of *meaning to convey*, which is central to understanding the intentionality of language, presupposes the further intentional concepts of *perceiving* and *endeavoring*.

Perceiving is a paradigm case of what we have called "indirectly believing," or "indirect attribution." In perceiving the car, say, to be moving, one directly attributes to oneself the property of being appeared to by just one thing and to a thing that is a car and moving. The intentional element is perceiving is this:

D3   x perceptually takes y to be F = Df y and only y appears G to x; and x directly believes of x the property of being appeared G to by just one thing and by a thing that is F

The ordinary concept of perception includes the further concept of *being evident*:

D4   x perceives y to be F = DF x perceptually takes y to be F; and it is evident to x that y is F

The intentional element in the concept of endeavor may be expressed by "The property of being F is such that x endeavors to have it." In some contexts, "acts *with the intention* of" will be used instead of "endeavors to." *Indirect* endeavor is analogous to indirect belief. (Once again, I will use "x believes himself to be F" as short for "x believes being-F directly of x.")

D5   x indirectly endeavors that y be F = Df There is a relation R such that:
(1) x will bear R just to y;

(2) the property of bearing R to just one thing and to a thing that is F is such that x endeavors to have it;

(3) x is more justified in believing himself to be such that he will bear R to just one thing than in not believing himself to be such that he will bear R to just one thing; and

(4) if x believes himself to be such that the thing he will bear R to is the thing he will bear S to, then he is at least as justified in believing himself to be such that he will bear R to just one thing as he is in believing himself to be such that he will bear S to just one thing

Our definition of *de re* endeavor is now this:

D6   x endeavors that y be F = Df Either (a) x is identical with y and endeavors to have the property being-F or (b) x indirectly endeavors that y be F

We need also the concept of endeavoring to do one thing *for the purpose* of bringing about another thing (or *in order to* bring about another thing). For present purposes this simplification will do:

D7   x endeavors to bring about P and does so *for the purpose* of bringing about q = Df x endeavors to bring it about that his endeavor to bring about P cause Q

This concept thus presupposes the concept of causation.

Meaning to Convey

The relation between thought and language may now be described by reference to the concept of *meaning to convey*. Meaning to convey is *endeavoring* to convey. What, then, is *conveying*? If I want to convey something to you, then I have a certain thought I want to communicate to you; and this means, in part, that there is something I want to cause you to think of. (I here take "cause to think of" broadly—to cover both the case where one is caused to *begin* to think of a certain thing and also the case where one is caused to *continue* to think of that thing.)

But conveying is more than merely causing to think of. Let us consider two cases of causing to think of that are not cases of conveying.

(1) I inject you with a certain drug that makes people paranoiac and then I present you to Mr. Jones. The result is that you believe that Mr. Jones desires to persecute you. But even if it had been my intention to cause you to believe this, we cannot say, taking "convey" in its present sense, that I have *conveyed* this to you.

(2) Kant cites the following case of intended deception that is not a case of lying: "I may wish people to think that I am off on a journey, and so I pack my luggage; people draw the conclusion I want them to draw. . . . I have not lied to them, for I have not stated that I am expressing my opinion." [4]

Kant's remark may suggest that, in order to be able to tell you anything, I must first tell you that I am going to tell you something, and in order to to be able to convey anything, I must first convey that I'm going to convey something. This type of regress would hardly be acceptable.

What, then, does *conveying* involve that mere *causing to think of* does not involve? I suggest that there are three marks that are characteristic of conveying but need not hold of mere causing to think of.

One mark of conveying may be illustrated by this: If I convey something to you, I do so by causing you to believe that *I* am thinking of that something. This is not what happens when, merely by injecting a drug, I cause you to have a certain belief.

Second, if I convey something to you, then my *purpose* in causing you to believe that I am thinking of the thing in question is that of causing *you* to think of that thing.

And a *third* mark of conveying pertains to the fact that one is *addressing* someone. If I mean to convey to you the thought that so-and-so, then I intend to cause you to believe that I *intend* to cause you to have the thought that so-and-so. Hence, conveying presupposes a complex belief situation. We must be able to say such things as: "x endeavors to cause y to believe that he, x, believes with respect to z that it is F."

Meaning to convey, then, presupposes the following concepts: making an utterance; causal contribution; perception; endeavor: thinking of; and belief. I will now say what it is to *address an utterance* for the *purpose* of conveying something. For simplicity, I will restrict myself to the situation wherein the speaker is addressing only one person; and I will use abbreviations introduced by previous definitions.

> D8 x addresses an utterance to z to convey the thought to z that y if F= Df
> (1) x makes an utterance so that z will perceive that utterance and thereby believe that x thinks of y as F; (2) x does this to cause z to believe that he, x, intends to cause z to think of y as F; and (3) his purpose in doing this is to cause z to think of y as F

When the conditions of the above definition are fulfilled, we may say that y is the *object* concerning which x means to convey something, and that the property of being F is the *content* of what it is that x means to convey with respect to y.

A broader concept may be obtained by revising the first clause of the definiens. Instead of saying that x intends to cause z to "believe that he, x, thinks of y as being F," we could say that x intends to cause z to "believe that there is a y such that he, x, thinks of y as being F." This would accommodate the situation (for example, a hallucination) wherein the belief has no intentional *object*.

Sense and Reference

If a person x believes, with respect to a thing y, that y has a certain property P, then y is the *object* of the belief in question and the property P is the *content*. In terms of this intentional distinction between content and object, we may now spell out the linguistic distinction between sense and reference.[5] The analysis of *sense* makes use of the concept of the *content* of thought, and the analysis of *reference*, or *designation*, makes use of the concept of the *object* of thought.

I will use the expression "attributive sense" in order to distinguish the concept in question from the kind of sense that is sometimes attributed to proper names and demonstratives.

We begin with the "speaker's sense" of a predicate:

D9 x uses P with the attributive sense S = DF x addresses an utterance for the purpose of conveying something, and P is that part of x's utterance which is intended to bring it about that S is the content of the thought he thus endeavors to cause

"Part" is here to be read as "proper part"; hence, if P is "that part of the utterance" which is intended to bring about so-and-so, then there will be *another* part of the utterance, discrete from P, which is *not* intended to bring about so-and-so. Hence, P cannot be identified with the entire utterance.

The concept of the "hearer's sense" is this:

D10 z interprets x's use of P as having the attributive sense S = Df z perceives that part of x's utterance which is P and believes of it that x meant to use it with the attributive sense S

I have spoken of the sense of predicative expressions—those utterances that are used to convey the *content* of one's thought. May we also ascribe a sense to such designative expressions as demonstratives and proper names?

We *could* ascribe a sense to proper names and demonstratives. For example, if I use a proper name in speaking to another person, then the demonstrative sense of that name on that occasion could be said to pertain to the relation or relations by means of which I then single out the object—or objects—of the belief I am expressing to the other person. Any such identifying relation will be a relation such that the bearer of the name is the thing to which the user of the name bears that relation. Consider again my statement "That green car is out of control." One could say that the demonstrative sense of my expression "that green car" might be the property expressed by "the green car I have just been watching." In this case, it would be the relational property of being someone who has just been watching one and only one green automobile.

The demonstrative sense of a name, then, would *not* be a property of the bearer of the name. It would be, rather, a relational property that the user of the name attributes to himself. The property, therefore, would be a property of the *user* of the name—provided there is a bearer of the name. And the corresponding relation would be one that the user of the name bears only to the bearer of the name.

But it is not clear that anything is to be gained by the introduction of this concept of demonstrative sense. For we do not need to use it in explicating the designative function of proper names and demonstratives.

What, then, of the concept of *designation*?

We first consider what may be called the "speaker's designation" of a word:

D11   x uses N to designate y = Df x makes an utterance for the purpose of thereby conveying something about y; and N is that part of x's utterance which is intended to bring it about that y is the object of the thought that x thus endeavors to cause

We have distinguished the case where one's thought *has* an object from the case where one's thought only *purports* to have an object. It was suggested that the latter situation may arise when I believe that there is one and only one person who is a devil and that that person is following me. Now it might be that I use the name "Satan" for this person. But we cannot say that I use "Satan" to *designate* him, for the person doesn't exist. Let us say that, in such a case, I "*mean* to use 'Satan' to designate something." The relevant concept is this:

D12   x means to use N to designate something = Df x makes an utterance for the purpose of thereby conveying something about a certain thing; and N is that part of x's utterance which is intended to bring it about that the thing, with respect to which he endeavors to convey this something, is the object of the thought he thus endeavors to convey

The concept defined in D11 implies that defined in D12, but not conversely.

We now turn to what might be called the "hearer's designation" of a word:

D13   z interprets x's use of N as designating y = Df z perceives that part of x's utterance which is N and believes of it that x meant to use it to designate y

Or z may simply interpret x's use of N as *purporting* to designate something. In such a case, z does not believe with respect to a thing y that x meant to use N to designate y; z believes only that x meant to use N to designate something.

Looking back to our account of designation, one may ask, "*How* does it happen that x's utterance of N can bring about the desired effect?" If x's utterance is successful, then there will be someone z who is caused to perceive N and in consequence to think of y. There is, therefore, a *causal* factor that is involved: x's utterance of N causes z to think of y. Hence there *can* be a "causal theory of meaning": that is to say, there can be a causal *explanation* of the fact that a person's perception of an utterance N, or part of such an utterance, causes him to think of a certain thing y. But this is not a causal theory of *what* it is for one to think of another thing—much less a causal theory of what it is for one thing to designate another thing.

I have, then, attempted to single out certain intentional concepts in terms of which we may define *sense* and *reference*. We must distinguish (1) the sense in which we can say of a certain word in English that it has a fixed sense and that, at any time, it can be used in English to designate only one specific type of object at that time; and (2) the sense in which we can of a certain word, say "John," that it is now used to designate John and now used to designate Mary. We have been concerned here with (2), with "speaker's meaning," and not with (1), not with "linguistic meaning." Linguistic meaning, so conceived, should be thought of as idealized speaker's meaning.

In this way, then, I would defend the principle of the primacy of the intentional.

Notes

1. I have defended a version of this view in *The First Person: An Essay on Reference and Intentionality* (Brighton and Minneapolis: Harvester Press and University of Minnesota Press, 1981).

2. This example is adapted from one suggested by Keith Donnellan in "Reference and Definite Descriptions," *Philosophical Review*, 75 (1966): 281–304.

3. Compare A. N. Whitehead's example of "That college building is commodius," in *The Concept of Nature* (Cambridge: The University Press, 1930), pp. 6–7.

4. *Lecture on Ethics* (New York: Harper & Row, 1963), p. 226. The German reads: " . . . dann habe ich ihn nicht belogen, denn ich habe nicht deklariert, meine Gesinnung zu äussern." See Paul Menzer (ed.), *Eine Vorlesung Kants uber Ethik* (Berlin: Rolf Heise, 1925), p. 286. Compare Roderick M. Chisholm and Thomas D. Feehan, "The Intent to Deceive," *Journal of Philosophy*, 74 (1977): 143–60.

5. Compare the distinction between "referential" and "attributive" in Keith Donnellan, "Reference and Definite Descriptions."

Part V
An Intentional Approach to Ontology

15

Properties and States of Affairs Intentionally Considered

Platonism

Are there such things as properties? There are many things that we *seem* to know about properties.

Some properties (for example, the property of being a horse) are exemplified; and some of them (for example, the property of being a unicorn) are not exemplified. Some of them (for example, the property of being both round and square) cannot be exemplified by anything. And some of them (for example, the property of being self-identical) must be exemplified by everything. There are properties P and Q that are necessarily so related that if P is exemplified, then Q is also exemplified. There are properties P and Q that are necessarily so related that if P is exemplified, then Q is *not* exemplified. Some properties P and Q are are so related that one cannot *conceive* P without also conceiving Q. And there are many other such a priori truths.

Is this knowledge really just a kind of knowledge about individual things and, therefore, strictly speaking, not about properties at all? And how are we to decide? If our ostensible knowledge of properties were just a kind of knowledge about individual things, then we could paraphrase our ostensible property statements into statements in which the individual terms and variables can be interpreted as taking only individual things as their values.

Certainly *some* of the statements expressing what we know about properties can be thus paraphrased. For example, "The property of being a horse is exemplified" can be put as "There exists an x such that x is a horse"; and "The property of being a unicorn is not exemplified" can be put as "It is false that there exists an x such that x is a unicorn."

But such paraphrase is not possible in every case. Consider the following statements: "There are shapes that are not exemplified"; "Certain pairs of properties are necessarily such that if one of the members is exemplified then the other is also exemplified"; and "Certain pairs of properties are necessarily such that it is impossible to conceive one of them without also conceiving the other." Such statements as these, so far as I can see, cannot be paraphrased into statements referring only to individuals.

This fact, I would say, constitutes at least a prima facie justification for accepting extreme realism: there *are* properties, some of which are exemplified and some of which are not exemplified.

The Question of the Structure of Properties

Properties have an intentional structure. Some are compound and some are noncompound. And of those that are compound, some are conjuctive, some are disjunctive, and some are negative. Thus *red and round* is compound and conjunctive; *red or round* is compound and disjunctive; and *nonred* is compound and negative.

Such a conception readily provokes the following objection. "You are mislead by the *language* we use to talk about properties. If a property — say, what you call 'red or round' — can be said to be 'disjunctive', then this simply reflects an incidental linguistic fact, the fact that the property can be expressed by means of a disjunctive predicate (a predicate made up of two noncompound predicates with a disjunction sign between them). And analogously for 'conjunctive', 'negative', and 'compound'. What you call the 'structure of properties' is nothing more than the structure of the *language* we use in formulating our predicates."

More particularly, one may raise such questions as these:

Is brother a noncompound property — or is it the conjunctive property of being male and a sibling?

What of the property of being a sibling? Is *it* a noncompound property — or is it the disjunctive property of being either a brother or a sister?

Is being human the disjunctive property of being either a man or a woman? Or is being a man the conjunctive property of being male and human, and is being a woman the conjunctive property of being female and human?

Is being mortal negative or affirmative? What, then, of being immortal?

You say that *red* is noncompound. But isn't it the same as the conjunctive property, *red and red*? And isn't it also the same as the disjunctive property, *red or red*, not to mention the disjunctive property of *being either red and round or red and nonround*?

One may be tempted to conclude, therefore, that the so-called structure of properties is simply a reflection of the kind of *language* we happen to use in expressing our thoughts about properties.

But let us look more closely at the nature of properties.

Basic Relations between Properties

We will first note certain ways in which properties may be related to each other.

(A) *Implication*:

One property may be said, in the following sense, to *imply* another;

D1 P implies Q = Df P is necessarily such that if it is exemplified then Q is exemplified

The property *being a wife* may be said, in this sense, to imply the property *being a husband*, and conversely. Each of the two properties is necessarily such that, if it is exemplified, then the other is exemplified. But the thing that exemplifies the one is not identical with the thing that exemplifies the other. Hence, we may single out a subspecies of property implication.

(B) *Inclusion*:

D2 P includes Q = Df P is necessarily such that whatever exemplifies it exemplifies Q

The property of being a dog includes that of being an animal: a thing cannot have the first property without also having the second. If one property includes another, then the first property also implies the second; but, as we have just seen, one property may imply another without including the other.

(C) *Involvement*:

We next introduce an important intentional relation that obtains between various properties: one property may be said to *involve* another.

Consider these four properties: (i) *being either red or round*; (ii) *being nonred*; (iii) *being possibly red*; and (iv) *wanting something that is red*. All these properties are intimately related to the property *being red*, yet they neither include nor imply it. They *involve* the property red in the following sense: each is necessarily such that it is impossible for one to conceive it without conceiving the property red. We will say, then:

D3 P involves Q = Df P is necessarily such that whoever conceives it conceives Q

The property of being *both* red *and* round involves the property of being round (for one cannot conceive it without conceiving the property of being round). And it also *implies* the property of being round. The property of being *either* red *or* round also involves the property of being round, but it does *not* imply the property of being round. So, too, for the property of being nonround: it involves but does not imply the property of being round. Again, the *intentional* property of wanting something that is red involves but does not imply the property of being red. Further, the *dispositional* property of being potentially red involves but does not imply the property of being red. And, finally, the *causal* property, preventing something from becoming red, involves but does not imply the property of being red. Thus many properties involve properties they do not imply.

And many properties imply properties they do not involve. *Being red*, for example, implies – but does not involve – *being either red or round*; it also implies but does not involve the property of *being either red and round or red and non-round*, as well as that of *being self-identical* and that of *being such that 7 and 5 are 12*.

(D) *Entailment*:

We define the relation of property *entailment* – in terms of attribution and necessity:

D4   P entails Q = Df P is necessarily such that, for every x and every y, if y attributes P to x, then y attributes Q to x

We assume that, if P entails Q, then P includes and involves Q. And we have noted that, if P includes Q, then P implies Q.

But it is possible for a property P both to include and to involve a property Q without thereby entailing Q (in the present sense of "entail"). The property of *being either both round and square or such that 7 and 5 are 13* includes and involves the property of *being both round and square*, but it does not entail that property. In other words: one cannot conceive the first property without conceiving the second; but one can attribute the first property to a thing without attributing the second property to anything. Again, the property *being red and either not colored or round* implies and involves the property of *being round*, but it does not entail that property.[1]

One property thus entails another only if the attribution of the first property implies the attribution of the second.

Identity Criteria for Properties

If, in contemporary philosophy, one discusses a type of entity that is not an individual thing, one is confronted with the question: "What *criteria of identity* are there for the type of entity you are discussing?"

Let us consider four possible criteria of property identity.

(1) The first is this: A property P is identical with a property Q if and only if whatever has P has Q and conversely. Adoption of this criterion would have the consequence that the property of being a rational animal is identical with that of being a featherless biped, and that the property of being a unicorn is identical with that of being a mermaid. It would also have the consequence that the property of being such that all men are mortal is identical with the property of being such that 7 and 5 are 12.

(2) A second possible criterion of property identity is this: P is identical with Q if and only if each of P and Q is *necessarily* such that whatever has it has the other. Or, in other words, P is identical with Q if and only if P and Q are *logically equivalent*. Adoption of this criterion would have the consequence that the property being an equilateral triangle is the same as the property of being an equiangular triangle. It would also have the consequence that the property of being red is

identical with the property of being either red and spherical or red and non-spherical.

(3) A third possible criterion of property identity is *intentional*: P is identical with Q if and only if P and Q both imply and involve each other. In such a case, they are necessarily such that if the one is exemplified then the other is exemplified, and also necessarily such that whoever conceives the one conceives the other. But this would require us to say that the property of *striking* is identical with the property of *being struck* and that the property of *killing* is identical with the property of *being killed*.

(4) Hence a more satisfactory intentional criterion would be one using mutual *inclusion* instead of *mutual implication*: P is identical with Q if and only if P and Q include and involve each other.

We will adopt this final intentional criterion of property identity. Consider now the following objection to our criterion.

"Surely the statement 'Red is the color of ripe strawberries' is a paradigmatic contingent statement of property identity. And yet it is one thing to think of a thing as being red and it is another thing to think of a thing as having the color of ripe strawberries. A person who does not know what color ripe strawberries have may be able to conceive the property red—but will not be able to conceive the color of ripe strawberries. Therefore your criterion of property identity is too strong."

We should distinguish (A) that property which, as it happens, is the color property that is exemplified by all ripe strawberies and (B) that property which is *being* that color property that is exemplified by all ripe strawberries. Property (A) is the property red; property (B) is not the property red, but a property that, as it happens, is exemplified by the property red. It is true that a person cannot conceive the property red unless he can conceive (A) that property which is the color property exemplified by all ripe strawberries. But the above objection presupposes, mistakenly, that a person cannot conceive the property red unless he can conceive (B) that property which is *being* the color property that is exemplified by all ripe strawberries. One *can* conceive the color property exemplified by all ripe strawberries without having any conception at all of a ripe strawberry.

It is one thing, then, to know that something has the color red, but it is another thing to know that something has the color of ripe strawberries. If you know that a thing has the color red, then you may deduce that the thing has a color that is necessarily such that, for every possible world, if a thing has that color in that world, then it is red in that world. But if you know that the thing has the color of ripe strawberries, then you may *not* deduce that the thing has a color that is necessarily such that for every possible world, if a thing has that color in that world, then it has the color of ripe strawberries in that world.[2]

I turn now to the intentional structure of properties.

Conjunctive and Disjunctive Properties

"Being red and being red" is a conjunctive *phrase*. But there is no point in saying that, in addition to the property being red, there is also the conjunctive property, *being red and being red*. We cannot distinguish conceiving *being red* from conceiving *being red and being red*. And, similarly, there is no point in saying that, in addition to the conjunctive property, *being red and round*, there is also the conjunctive property, *being round and red*; nor is there reason to say that there is also the property *being round and red and round*.

We have said that a property P *entails* a property Q, provided only that for every x and y, if x attributes P to y, then x attributes Q to y.

I will say that a *conjunctive* property is a property that entails two properties and that is implied by everything that implies those two properties. (Since we speak of *two* properties, neither will entail the other.) The two properties are the *conjuncts* of the conjunction.

The definition is:

D5   C is the conjunction of P and Q = Df (1) C entails P; (2) C entails Q; (3) P does not entail Q; (4) Q does not entail P; and (5) everything entailed by C entails something that either P or Q entails

The property *red and round* will thus be a conjunction of the properties *red* and *round*. But it will not be a conjunction of *red* and *both round and self-identical*, for the property *red* does not entail the latter property.

I assume that for any two properties not related by entailment, there is that property which is their conjunction.

A *disjunctive* property is a property that is related in the following way to two other properties: it involves them but does not entail them, and it is necessarily such that it is exemplified by a thing only if the thing has one or the other of the two properties. The two properties are its *disjuncts*.

D6   D is a disjunction of G and H = Df (i) D involves but does not entail G, and D involves but does not entail H; (ii) G does not entail H, and H does not entail G; and (iii) D is necessarily such that, for every x, x has D, if and only if either x has G or x has H

The reference to entailment in this definition has as a consequence that such expressions as the following do not connote disjunctive properties: "either red or both red and round."

I assume that for any two properties that are not related by entailment there is that property which is their disjunction.

Negations of Properties

We turn now to the following two concepts: that of the *negation* of a property and also that of a *negative* property. The definitions I shall propose have the following two consequences: (1) the property of *being red* has as its (only) negation the property of *being nonred*; and (2) the property of *being nonred* is a *negative* property and the property of *being red* is *not* a negative property.

Let us first mark off the notion of property contradiction:

> D7 P contradicts Q = Df P is necessarily such that, for every x, x exemplifies P if and only if x does not exemplify Q

Red thus stands in the relation of contradiction with its negation, *nonred*. But it also stands in the relation of contradiction with many properties other than its negation; these are such complex properties as *nonred and self-identical*, and *either (nonred and round) or (nonred and not round)*. Given our criterion of property identity, we cannot say that these more complex properties are identical with the property *nonred*.

What, then, is distinctive about the relation between *nonred* and *red*? Not only does *nonred* contradict *red*; it also "properly involves" it—that is to say, *nonred* involves *red*, but *red* does not involve *nonred*. Moreover, *nonred*, unlike the complex properties cited above, does not properly involve anything that both contradicts and properly involves *red*. Let us use these marks to define a *negative contradictory* of a property:

> D8 P is the negation of Q = Df (1) P contradicts Q; (2) P involves Q; and (3) Q does not involve P

We may now say that a *negative property* is a property that is the negation of a property.

We may note still another mark of negative properties: A negative property does not entail any property other than itself. And if a negative property (say, nonred) is one such that its regation (red) is not necessary to anything, then the negative property is possibly such that everything has it.

Negative properties are sometimes referred to as infinite properties—the thought being, I think, that a negative property is a property that is possibly such that everything has it. This is true of *nonred*, but it is not true of *nonself-identical*, which would be negative according to our definition.

Earlier Questions about Structure

We now return to those questions which expressed doubts about the concept of the *intentional structure* of properties. The answers are clear.

Is the property of *being a brother* a conjunctive property? It is. One of its conjuncts is *being male*; the other conjunct is *having the same parents that someone else has*.

Is the property of *being a sibling* a disjunction property? No. It is identical with that of *having the same parents that someone else has*. Hence, it is noncompound and therefore not a disjunctive property.

The property of *being a man* is the conjunctive property of *being a male and being human*. Being a sibling, therefore, is noncompound and, hence, not a disjunctive property.

The property of *being mortal* is the property of being such that one is going to die. And the property of *being immortal* is the conjunction of *being alive* and *not being mortal*. Hence, being mortal is a noncompound affirmative property; and being immortal is a conjunction of a noncomound affirmative property and a noncompound negative property.

States of Affairs

The term "states of affairs" in *one* of its various uses refers to a type of abstract object that is at least analogous in many respects to properties. Properties may be divided into those that are *exemplified* and those that are *not exemplified*. There *are*, therefore, properties that are *not exemplified*. And states of affairs may be divided, analogously, into those that *obtain* and those that do *not* obtain. There *are*, therefore, states of affairs that *do not obtain*.

Is it possible, then, that states of affairs, so conceived, constitute a subspecies of property? We might be tempted to say that the state of affairs *that-p* is to be identified with the property of *being-such-that-p*. But *is* there such a property as "being such that p"? What we should say is, rather, this:

D9 That-p is a state of affairs = Df There is a property which is necessarily such that it is exemplified if and only if p

This definition guarantees that states of affairs are abstract things and not contingent events. For properties are necessary things and therefore if a property can be said to be *"necessarily* such that p," then the sentence replacing "p" in the expression "that-p is a state of affairs" cannot express a contingent event.

Since states of affairs are thus reducible to properties, the expression "the state of affairs that-p *obtains*" is reducible to a statement about *exemplification*:

D10 The state of affairs that-p obtains = Df Something has a property which is necessarily such that it is exemplified only if p

What of *propositions*? If we use "proposition" to refer to a type of abstract object and not to a type of contingent thing (such as those "singular propositions" that are thought to contain contingent things as their constituents), then there would seem to be no ground for distinguishing propositions from states of affairs—unless we say that propositions are those states of affairs which are necessarily such that either they are always exemplified or they are never exemplified. And the concept of the *truth* of a proposition would be explicated by reference to exemplification in the way in which *obtaining* is explicated above.

And so our analyses of the intentional structures of properties may also be interpreted as analyses of the intentional structures of *states of affairs* or abstract *propositions*. The schematic letters in the definitions of property *conjunction*

(D5), property *disjunction* (D6), and property *negation* (D7) may be replaced by terms for states of affairs.

Frege raises the question whether there can be a distinction between *affirmative* and *negative* states of affairs (in his terminology, affirmative and negative thoughts) and he concludes: "For logic at any rate such a distinction is wholly necessary: its ground must be sought outside logic. I know of no logical principle where verbal expression makes it necessary to use these terms."[3] Yet there is a valid distinction to be made. If we assume that every state of affairs has one and only one negation, then we may say this: a state of affairs is *affirmative* if and only if it does not involve its own negation; otherwise it is *negative*. Hence, for every state of affairs and its negation, one will be negative and the other affirmative.

Notes

1. Compare the distinction between the "entertainment" and the "doxastic" senses of propositional entailment in Roderick M. Chisholm, "Events, Propositons, and States of Affairs," in P. Weingartner and E. Morscher (eds.), *Ontologie und Logik* (Berlin: Duncker und Humblot, 1979), pp. 27–47; see esp. p. 31.

2. Compare Wittgenstein's observation: "It is easy to see that not all colour concepts are logically of the same sort, e.g., the difference between the concepts 'colour of gold' or 'colour of silver' and 'yellow' or 'grey.' " *Remarks on Colour* (Berkeley: University of California Press, 1978), p. 9e.

3. Gottlob Frege, in Peter Geach and Max Black (eds.), *Translations from the Philosophical Writings of Gottlob Frege* (Oxford: Basil Blackwell, 1952). The quotation is from p. 125 of "Negation."

16

States and Events

Aristotle and Bolzano had said that some things are beings *of* other things.[1] We will say that if one thing is a being *of* another thing, then the first thing is *a state of* the second. And we will take "x is a state of y" as undefined. In this way, we will be able to set forth an explication of *events* and to show how events are related to attributes and to individual things.

The Logical Properties of States

Our assumption that there are states of things may be put this way:

> A1 For every x, there is the state x-being-F if and only if x exemplifies being-F

We thus use "being-F" as a term to designate attributes and "x-being-F" as a term to designate states. The letter "F" may be replaced by any well-formed English predicate; and "x" in "x-being-F" designates the entity having the state that is designated by "x-being-F."

As a being *of* another thing, a state is not an *ens per se*. We may express this fact by saying that states are ontologically dependent on the things of which they *are* states:

> A2 For every x and y, if x is a state of y, then x is necessarily such that it is a state of y

Even the contingent states of a thing are necessarily such that they are states of that thing. A person who is sad is not necessarily such that he is sad; but his-being-sad is necessarily such that it is a state of him.

Those contingent things that are not states of other things may be called *individual things*.

"Particular States"

A thing may be said to enter into temporal or causal relations *via* its states. For example, we may say of a person that his falling contributes causally to his being injured. The cause of the injury was a "particular fall" that the person had and the effect was a "particular injury." How are we to describe this situation? It was not just the attribute of falling that contributed to the injury; it was a certain particular fall and a certain particular injury — a fall that can be individuated and an injury that can be individuated.

Must we distinguish, then, as Stout did, between universals as abstract objects and universals as particulars? No — for, making use of the concept of a state and expressing ourselves in a language that is tensed, we may individuate the fall and the injury in another way.

I will not assume, as many contemporary philosophers do, that there *are* such things as "*times*." And, therefore, I will not assume that there are things designated by those linguistic expressions that are *dates* — for example, "June 3, 1988." I do assume, of course, that things persist: some things *had* attributes that they no longer have; and some things *will have* attributes that they do not have. And from this it follows that some states are temporally preceded by other states and that some states are temporally followed by other states.

I will now describe a way of *individuating* states without presupposing the concept of time. I will single out certain attributes that may be called "temporally denumerable."

A *temporally denumerable* attribute has two distinct features: (1) it is an attribute that is necessarily such that whatever has it has it only *once*; yet (2) it has a *content* that is repeatable. Hence, we must make clear what is here intended by the expressions "only once" and "repeatable content."

We presuppose that there are things that have come into being and that there are things that will pass away. In "Coming into Being and Passing Away," we discussed what it is for a thing to come into being and for a thing to pass away. Using tense, we said that a thing *is coming into being* provided only it is such that there is nothing it did exemplify; and we said that a thing *has just passed away* provided that something that was such that the thing exists is beginning to be such that it does not exist. We add, then, this principle:

A3   There exists an x which is such that either x is coming into being or did come into being; and there exists or will exist a y which is or will be such that x has just passed away

Now we may give a sense to such expressions as "the first time," "the second time," and "the n-th time," and do so without reference to times.

D1   x is F for the first time = Df (1) x is F; and (2) x is not such that it was both non-F and such that it had been F x is F for at least the n-th time = Df (1) x is F; and (2) x was both non-F and such that it had been F for the (n-1) time

x is F for not more than the n-th time = Df (1) x is F; and (2) it is false that x was both non-F and such that it had been F for at least the n-th time

x is F for the n-th time = Df (1) x is F for at least the n-th time; and (2) x is F for not more than the n-th time

And analogously for "the last time," "at least one more time after this," "at most one more time after this," and so on.

Now we may say what a "temporally denumerable" attribute is:

D2 P is a temporally denumerable attribute of x = Df x has P; there is a finite number n and an attribute Q which are necessarily such that: for every y, y has P if and only if, either y has Q for the n-th time or y will have Q n more times

The attribute Q may be said to be the "repeatable content" of the attribute P.

For example, if I am lecturing for the 700th time, then the attribute of lecturing for the 700th time is a temporally denumerable attribute that has as its content the repeatable attribute of lecturing. Or if I will lecture just 37 times after this, then the attribute of being as to give that lecture which is my 38th lecture before my final one is a temporally denumerable attribute that has the attribute of lecturing as its repeatable content.

Definition of Event

We have assumed that for every x, x is F if and only if there is the attribute being-F and there is the state x-being-F. Now we may say what it is for a state to be an event.

D3 x-being-F is an event = Df (1) x is F; and (2) the attribute being-F is a temporally denumerable attribute that only individuals can have and that nothing has necessarily

One may object: "Your definition is adequate to those events involving just one thing. But what of events involving a great multiplicity of things — events such as hurricanes, wars, and revolutions?" If we think of aggregates of individuals as being themselves individuals, then we may say that such events are states of aggregates of individuals.

I make use, therefore, of the concept "x is part of y," and add the following principle, which has the same content as Lesniewski's principle concerning "sums" of individuals:

A5 If x and y are contingent individuals and have no parts in common, then there is a contingent individual composed of x and y

This tells us, in effect, that *heaps, aggregates,* or *sums* of individuals are themselves individuals. Hurricanes, wars, and revolutions may thus be thought of as states of sums of individuals.[2]

Recurrence

Events are entities that are contingent, for they are terms of the relation of causation and terms of such temporal relations as before and after. Yet the theory of causation and the theory of probability require us to say that events may *recur*. What would it mean to say, of a contingent thing, that *it* may recur?

The question is especially difficult if we accept Locke's dictum according to which nothing can "have two beginnings of existence." Recurrence, one might suppose, is a property of *attributes*; attributes, we have said, are noncontingent things.

What, then, of *recurrence*? I suggest the following:

D4   x-being-F is recurring = Df x is F; and x was such that it was both non-F and such as to have been F

Strictly speaking, therefore, what recurs are not events but rather those attributes that constitute the repeatable contents of events.

Negative Attributes and Negative States

Given our assumption that there are states, we need not also assume that there are "facts." For states perform all the theoretical functions commonly assigned to facts. Hence, we do not have the problem of explicating "negative facts."

But there are *negative attributes* — for example, the attribute nongreen. And therefore there are *negative states* — for example, this piece of paper being nongreen. Every negative state is a state of some entity and, like every other state, presupposes an entity that is not a state.

A *negative state*, then, has as its content a negative attribute. And what is a negative attribute? I am convinced that, to answer such a question, we must consider attributes from an *intentional* point of view.

Viewing attributes intentionally, we may say that the defining mark of an *attribute* is this: it is a thing that is possibly such that there is someone who attributes it to something. And we should note that attributes may be related in several different ways.

We may say that an attribute *implies* another attribute if the first attribute is necessarily such that if anything has it, then something has the second attribute. And we may say that an attribute *includes* another attribute if the first attribute is necessarily such that whatever has it also has the second.

Let us speak again of the "*involvement*" of attributes. Consider the four attributes: (i) *being either red or round*; (ii) *being nonred*; (iii) *being possibly red*; and (iv) *wanting something that is red*. All these attributes are intimately related to the attribute *being red*, yet they neither include nor imply it. Let us say that they *involve* the attribute red and try to say what involvement is. Once again we find the general idea suggested by Bolzano. He cites these examples: the concept of *a land without mountains* and that of *a book without engravings*. Bolzano does not use the term "involves" but puts the relationship by saying that "the parts of the idea [*die Teile der Vorstellung*]" need not be "*parts of the object [Teile des Gegenstandes]*."[3]

The attribute of *being a land without mountains* may be said, in the following sense, to *involve* the attribute *being a mountain*: it is impossible for anyone to conceive it without also conceiving the attribute *being a mountain*. And the four attributes just cited, which involve the attribute *being red*, do so in the following sense: each is such that it is impossible for anyone to conceive it without also conceiving the attribute red.

Now we are in a position to distinguish between attributes that are positive and attributes that are negative. The distinction between positive and negative is not a function of the fact that we use negative expressions such as "non" or "not" in connection with just one of the two expressions; it is not a linguistic distinction at all. It has to do, rather, with the structure or inner nature of the attributes themselves.

Let us distinguish attributes that *exclude* each other from attributes that *contradict* each other. Red may be said to *exclude* yellow in that it is impossible for anything to be *both* red and yellow. But it is possible for a thing to be *neither* red nor yellow. Red *contradicts* nonred in that it is necessary that everything is either red or nonred and it is impossible that anything is both. Hence, if two attributes contradict each other, then they also exclude each other; but they may exclude each other without contradicting each other.

Now we may say what it is for an attribute to be a negative attribute.

D5 Being-F is a negative attribute = Df One cannot conceive an attribute that excludes being-F without conceiving an attribute that contradicts being-F

In other words, if being-F is a negative attribute, then a contradictory of being-F is involved in every attribute that excludes being-F. *Red* is involved in every attribute that excludes *nonred*; but *nonred* is not involved in every attribute that excludes *red*. (*Yellow* excludes *being red*, and a person who cannot conceive *red* may be able to conceive *yellow*.)

Are There Negative Events?

The expression "negative event" may be taken in two ways. (1) It may be taken to refer to an event "that does not occur"; or (2) it may be taken to refer to an event having a negative content. If we take it in the first way, we need not say that there are negative events. But if we take it in the second way, we should say that there are negative events.

(1) Why would one think that there *are* "events that do not occur"? The *reason* for thinking this may be suggested by the following argument:

(1) The dam in the river prevented a serious flood

Therefore

(2) There was something that the dam prevented

Hence

(3) This something was an event

But

(4) That event did not occur

Therefore

(5) There was an event that did not occur

Step (2) of the argument is unjustified. For (1) does not tell us that there *is*, or *was*, something that the dam prevented. It tells us only that the dam caused that *negative state* which was the river not being such as to flood. This negative state is not "an event that does not occur"; it is an event with a negative content.

(2) We should say, then, that there *are* events having negative contents. There is, for example, that event which is this piece of paper having the negative attribute of nonblue.

"But do you need to speak of such events? This paper would not have the negative attribute nonblue unless it had some positive attribute—in the present case, the attribute of being white—that logically excludes the negative attribute. Doesn't the positive event—this piece of paper being white—serve all the theoretical purposes of the negative event?"

The objection presupposes that, if an *individual thing* has a negative attribute, then it has some positive attribute that logically excludes the contradictory of the negative attribute. But this presupposition is false. This may be seen most clearly in the case of *psychological* events. A person may have the negative attribute of not believing that it is raining in Graz; and the person may have that negative attribute without thereby having some positive attribute that excludes the contradictory of the negative attribute. Indeed, being such as *not* to be thinking is *not* a state that one has in virtue of any positive state that logically excludes the attribute of thinking.

Notes

1. "Every thing that there is is of one or the other of the following two types: either it is an entity which is *of* another thing [*an etwas Anderem*] or it exists, as one is accustomed to saying, *in itself* [*für sich*]." Bernard Bolzano, *Athanasia oder Gründe für die Unsterblichkeit der Seele* (Sulzbach: J. G. v. Seidelschen Buchhandlung, 1838), p. 21.

2. The present approach to events is obviously very close to that developed by Jaegwon Kim. See, for example, his "Events as Property Exemplifications," in Myles Brand and D. Walton (eds.), *Action Theory* (Dordrecht: D. Reidel, 1976), pp. 159–77. Events, Kim says, are "exemplifications by substances of properties at a time"; an event is a "structure consisting of a substance (an n-tuple of substances), a property (an n-adic relational property) and a time" (p. 160). But our account differs from that of Kim in that we do not presuppose that there are such entities as *times*.

3. *Theory of Science*, ed. Rolf George (Oxford: Basil Blackwell, 1972), p. 79. Compare Hugo Bergmann's *Das philosophische Werk Bernard Bolzanos* (Halle: Max Niemeyer, 1909), p. 40.

17

The Self in Austrian Philosophy

Bolzano's definition of *substance* provides us with a kind of key to the conceptions of the self in Austrian philosophy. His definition is as clear as anyone could possibly wish. He says that there are two kinds of things: (1) those things that are states or conditions of other things ("Beschaffenheiten von anderen Dingen"); and (2) those things that are not states or conditions of other things: "the latter are what I call *substances*."[1] Examples of things that are states or conditions of other things are "the color, smell and weight of a body," the beliefs that a particular person has, the sensations that he has, and the actions that he performs. Examples of substances—of things that are not states or conditions of other things—are physical bodies and selves.

Bolzano says, in Leibnizian fashion, that, if there are things that *are* states or conditions of other things, then there are things that are *not* states or conditions of other things.[2] If we use the term "substance" in the way he suggests, then we need not ask *whether* a given philosopher believes in substances; we need ask only *what* the things are that function for him as substances.

Sometimes Bolzano uses the word "property [*Eigenschaft*]" instead of "state or condition [*Beschaffenheit*]". But as he realizes, this is somewhat misleading. Acting, believing, and sensing *are* properties of me; but the actions that I perform and the beliefs and sensations that I have are *Beschaffenheiten* and not properties of me. One may say, for example, "Jones's sadness caused him to weep." This tells us, of course, that Jones does have the property of *being sad*. But it should not be taken to say that the property of being sad is what caused him to weep. It tells us rather that that state or *Beschaffenheit* which is *his being sad*—his having the property of being sad—is what caused him to weep. I would say that properties, as distinguished from states and conditions, are abstract objects and that the Platonist is right in calling them substances—provided he takes "substance" in

Bolzano's sense. A person's states or conditions—his *Beschaffenheiten*—are contingent things, dependent for their existence upon the person who is in them.

Such distinctions are obviously fundamental to the theory of the self.

Thus we may distinguish four quite different moments in Austrian philosophy. (1) There is the view of the metaphysicians that the self is a substance. (2) There is the view of early Austrian positivism that the self is not a substance but only a *Beschaffenheit*. (3) There is that phase of Austrian philosophy in which the self and its *Beschaffenheiten* are almost completely ignored. And finally, (4) there is the somewhat embarrassed *Wiederbekanntmachen* of Austrian philosophy and the self.

The Self as Substance

The self is a *simple substance* according to Bolzano.[3] He speaks of "our soul [*unsre Seele*]," but I believe that, strictly speaking, he would say, not that I *have* a soul, but that I *am* a soul.

Franz Brentano's view is very much like that of Bolzano. There is no problem in transforming Brentano's terminology of "substance and accident" into that of "substance and *Beschaffenheit*." He says that a substance is *in* its accidents, and it is natural to say, of course, that a thing is *in* its states. For Brentano and Marty, as we know, the psychological properties of the self constitute the key to all of metaphysics. I would say that their view has at least this much plausibility: the self is the only contingent substance with respect to which we have nontrivial certainty.

Meinong provides a variation upon this theme which recurs in subsequent Austrian philosophy. Exaggerating only a little, we could say that, according to Meinong, the *Beschaffenheiten* of the self provide us with the primary objects of philosophical investigation, but the self—that which has those *Beschaffenheiten*—is of no importance at all. Psychological properties—judging, assuming, sensing, perceiving, abstracting, comparing—provide Meinong with most of his subject matter and constitute his principal philosophical interest. And selves are, by definition, the things that have such properties. But Meinong shows no interest whatever in what it is that has the properties that only selves can have. Unlike Mach, he is not concerned to explain the self away or to reduce it to other entities; he simply ignores it.

We now turn to the second moment.

The Self as *Beschaffenheit*

Ernst Mach claims to dispense with the concept of substance. But if we take "substance" in Bolzano's sense, it would be more accurate to say that, according to Mach, the *substances* of the world are the things that Mach calls "elements"—namely, sensations. Physical things are complexes of sensations and so is the self.

What does it *mean* to say that the self is a complex of sensations? Mach expresses himself this way: "The elements *form* the self. To say that *I* sense green is only to say that the element green occurs in a certain complex of other elements."[4] His view is that any truth that may seem to be a truth about me is really a truth about certain sensations.

There are two serious difficulties with this version of the "bundle theory."

The first difficulty is that it is more of a promissory note than a theory; and Mach gives us no directions for cashing it in. He seems to be saying that statements about physical bodies and statements about selves can be derived from statements about sensations or complexes of sensations. What, then, of such simple statements as "There is a brown dog" and "Some people are philosophers"? How are they to be derived from statements about sensations? Mach gives us no answer and leaves us completely in the dark. We now know, what may have been less obvious a hundred years ago, that the program of reducing statements about physical things to statements about sensations involves difficulties in principle. No one has found a way of overcoming these difficulties.

The second difficulty with Mach's version of the bundle theory of the self is of a rather different sort. It is that of providing an answer to the question, "*Which* sensations constitute the elements?" There are three ways of interpreting Mach and none of them is satisfactory.

(1) According to one possible interpretation, your sensations and mine are simply "fictions" or "thought objects"; they are two construction steps away from those sensations that Mach finds to be the elements of the world. But you and I know that this view is false. At least *I* know that *my* sensations are not constructions upon Mach's sensations.

(2) The second way of interpreting Mach is solipsistic: there is only one self. So far as this possibility is concerned, the most reasonable comment is still that of Thomas Reid: "A traveller of good judgment may mistake his way, and be unawares led into a wrong track, and while the road is fair before him, he may go on without suspicion and be followed by others; but when it ends in a coal-pit, it requires no great judgment to know that he hath gone wrong, nor perhaps to find out what misled him."[5]

(3) According to the third way of interpreting Mach, *your* sensations are, *for him*, fictions or thought objects, and *his* sensations are, *for you*, fictions or thought objects. But this answer – with its "for him" and "for you" – reintroduces the concept of the self.

The problem, in a word, is this. We are provided with no way of deriving ordinary statements about the self from statements about the elements. And if we are told that, all the same, selves *are* bundles of sensations, then we have to have a way of distinguishing that bundle which is you from that bundle which is me. As Brentano had said in his lectures on descriptive psychology, the concept of a bundle requires that of "a cord or wire, or the like, that ties things together."[6] Without such a cord or wire, the contents of your bundle would spill over into mine. And no such cord or wire is at hand.

It is interesting to note that Ehrenfels, who was very much concerned with the self and its *Beschaffenheiten*, also flirts with the bundle theory. He said in his *Kosmogonie* that "substantialism" leads to serious philosophical problems. His thought seems to have been that, if we can emancipate ourselves from substantialism, then we can avoid the doctrine of the complete ineffectuality of the psychical.[7] Where Mach thinks of the self as a bundle of sensations, Ehrenfels says that it is a bundle of *properties [Eigenschaften]*. Like Mach, he doesn't tell us how the different bundles are to be distinguished from each other.

Ignoring the Self and Returning to Its *Beschaffenheiten*

With the advent of physicalism, the self and its *Beschaffenheiten* seem to be ignored. But it does not take long for the latter to return to the center of the stage.

Consider Schlick, for example. He ridicules the Cartesian *cogito* and suggests that the first-person pronoun cannot be used in expressing what is given in immediate experience. Yet when he tells us more about the nature of this experience, he makes essential use of the first-person pronoun.

In his essay "Über das Fundament der Erkenntnis" (1934), he compares what he calls "observation statements" with analytic statements. Observation statements and analytic statements, he says.

> have in common that the occasion of understanding them is the same as that of verifying them [*daß bei beiden der Vorgang des Verstehens zuleich der Vorgang der Verifikation ist*]; I grasp their meaning at the same time as I grasp their truth [*mit dem Sinne erfasse ich zugleich die Wahrheit*]. . . . Both are absolutely valid. However, while the analytic, tautological statement is empty of content, the observation statement supplies us with the satisfaction of genuine knowledge of reality [*echter Wirlichkeitserkenntnis*].[8]

He goes on to say that an observation statement might be expressed by saying something like "Here now blue" or "Here now yellow." But there was this objection: "Here now blue" and "Here now yellow" are not well-formed sentences; they contain no verb, copula or quantifier; and the predicates "blue" and "yellow" seem to function as terms. The year after the publication of his paper, Schlick deals with this objection. An observation statement, he says, tells us something like this: "There is something which is such that I believe I have used 'yellow' in the past to refer to that sort of thing and which is here now."[9] Further refinements are necessary.[10] But it is now clear that Schlick's observation statements are statements about the self.

So Austrian philosophy stumbles on the self once again.

Once we formulate our observation statements in the way Schlick proposes, we see that there is a large class of *psychological* statements all having the epistemological character associated with his observation statements. These are the statements expressing what the members of the Brentano school had called "inner perception"—statements beginning with such expressions as "I wish that," "I wonder whether," "I seem to see that," "I feel that."

Combining the terminologies of Meinong and Bolzano, we may say that such statements express *self-presenting Beschaffenheiten* of the self. It is these *Beschaffenheiten* and not sense-data or sense-qualities that constitute the objects of direct presentation or acquaintance. And when they are presented, then, as Brentano holds, the self is presented *nebenbei*—as that *of which* they are *Beschaffenheiten*.

Whatever the ontological elements may be, the epistemological elements are certain facts about the self.

And what of Wittgenstein? I would say that he gets us back on the road. The *Philosophical Investigations* is, of course, a treatise on certain *Beschaffenheiten* of the self. And a positive theory of consciousness is essential to the doctrine of the *Tractatus*. Wittgenstein does discuss the self there, but he doesn't say enough. I am thinking of this passage (5.641):

> There is therefore really a sense in which in philosophy one can speak non-psychologically of the I [*nicht-psychologisch vom Ich die Rede sein kann*]. The I occurs in philosophy through the fact that "the world is my world". The philosophical I is not the man, not the human body or the human soul [*Seele*] of which psychology treats, but the metaphysical subject, the limit—not a part of the world.

Wittgenstein does not elaborate. We don't know how this view is to be compared with that of Mach.

I would not say it to Wittgenstein myself, but if I were Bolzano I would speak to him this way: "Herr Kollege, Sie wissen ja, daß worüber man nicht schweigen kann, darüber muß man sprechen."

I wish that Wittgenstein had said more. For any plausible interpretation of what he did say has the consequence that the self—*das Ich*—is not one of those things that are *Beschaffenheiten* of other things.

I look forward to seeing where Austrian philosophy goes next.

Notes

1. Bolzano, *Athanasia oder Gründe für die Unsterblichkeit der Seele* (Sulzbach: J. G. v. Seidleschen Buchhandlung, 1838), p. 283.

2. Bolzano (1827), p. 22. He holds that *Beschaffenheiten* may themselves *have Beschaffenheiten* and that such things as numbers also have *Beschaffenheiten* (p. 22), and he seems to hold that God has a *Beschaffenheit* (p. 22).

3. Bolzano (1827), pp. 22, 53. He also argues, convincingly, that there is no problem involved in attributing spatial location to a simple substance (pp. 53, 287). He discusses this question further in the *Paradoxes of the Infinite*, Secs. 55-57. There is a brief reference to the distinction between substance and *Beschaffenheit* in *Wissenschaftslehre*, Sec. 142.

4. "Die Elemente *bilden* das Ich. *Ich* empfinde Grün, will, sagen daß das Element Grün in einem gewissen Complex von anderen Elementen (Empfindungen, Erinnerungen) vorkommt." *Beiträge zur Analyse der Empfindungen* (Jena: G. Fischer, 1886), Sec. 17.

5. *An Inquiry into the Human Mind*, Chap. 1, Sec. 8.

6. "Zum 'Bündel', wenn man es genau nimmt, gehört ein Strick oder Draht oder sonst etwas, was zusammenschnürt." *Deskriptive Psychologie* (Hamburg, Felix Meiner Verlag, 1982), p. 11.

7. Christian von Ehrenfels, *Kosmogonie* (Jena: Diedrichs, 1916), pp. 59ff, 77ff.

8. Moritz Schlick, "The Foundations of Knowledge," in A. J. Ayer (ed.), *Logical Positivism* (Glencoe, Ill.: Free Press, 1959), pp. 209–27; the quotation appears on p. 225. The original version of the paper, "Über das Fundament der Erkenntnis," may be found in Schlick's *Gesammelte Aufsätze* (Vienna: Gerold, 1938), pp. 289–310; the German version of the quotation appears on pp. 308–9.

9. "In our example, if the sentence 'Yellow here' stands for an affirmation [observation statement], then 'yellow' means 'the colour I remember always to have called "yellow" '. If so, there [may indeed be] a deception of memory, but even in this case the affirmation remains true (so long as a lie is not in question). Its truth does not depend on how I have otherwise really employed the words, but only on how I *think* at this moment that I have employed them. But I cannot be mistaken about that; as shown earlier, it is impossible for me not to have known this." From "Introduction and on 'Affirmations'," in M. Schlick, *Philosophical Papers*, vol. 2 (Dordrecht: D. Reidel, 1972), p. 412. This article is a selection from Schlick's *Sur le Fondement de la Connaissance* (Paris: Herman & cie, 1935).

10. I have discussed the question in more detail in "Schlick on the Foundations of Empirical Knowing," *Grazer Philosophische Studien*, 16/17 (1982): 149–57.

18

The Categories

> A *substance*—that which is called a substance most strictly, primarily, and most of all—is that which is neither said *of* a subject nor *in* a subject, e.g., the individual man or the individual horse. (Aristotle, *Categories*, Chap. 5.)

We present finally a classification of the most fundamental ontological categories. The classification will refine some of the concepts introduced in earlier essays. There will be four dichotomies—four ways of dividing sets of things into exclusive and exhaustive subsets. In each case, one of the two subsets will be the negation of the other. I will also attempt, so far as possible, to characterize each subset in positive terms.

The dichotomies are these:

(1) Things that are *contingent* and things that are noncontingent or *necessary*; (2) contingent things that are *states* and those that are nonstates or *contingent individuals*; (3) contingent individuals that are *limits* and those that are nonlimits or *contingent substances*; and (4) noncontingent things that are *abstracta* and those that are nonabstracta or *noncontingent substances*.

A Table of Categories

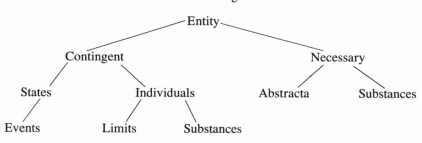

According to this way of looking at the world, then, there are contingent substances along with their states and their boundaries or limits; and there are necessary things, each of which is either an abtractum or a substance. I believe we have no good reason to affirm the existence of any *other* type of thing.

The Basic Concepts

Among the principal desiderata in thus setting forth a theory of categories are (1) economy with respect to the types of entity which are countenanced and (2) simplicity with respect to the types of concept which are used.

I will make use of these undefined concepts: (1) x *exemplifies* (has) y; (2) x is *necessarily* such that it is F; (3) x is a *state* of y; (4) x is a *constituent* of y; and (5) x *attributes* y to z. I will introduce three types of term: (1) "*being-F*," wherein the letter "F" may be replaced by any well-formed English predicate; (2) "*x-being-F*," which will be used to designate *states* of the entity designated by "x"; and (3) "*that-p*," in which the letter "p" may be replaced by any well-formed English sentence. And I will make essential use of *tense*. For I assume that there are truths that can be adequately expressed only in a language that, like our ordinary language, is tensed.

Since I am using tensed language, I will say that whatever exists exists now. And since the language *is* tensed, the "now" in "Whatever exists exists now" is redundant and the statement is logically true. But there *was* a philosopher who drank the hemlock. And this means that there *is* something—for example, the property of being blue—that *was* such as to have the property of being such that there *is* a philosopher who is drinking the hemlock.

I now turn to the four dichotomies.

(1) Contingent and Necessary Things

How are we to distinguish between those things that are contingent and those things that are not?

We have the locution "x is necessarily such that it is F." But unfortunately we cannot use this locution to make the distinction between necessary and contingent things. For "is necessarily such that it is F," at least as I interpret it, is equivalent to "is necessarily such that it exists if and only if it is F." And if the locution is taken in this way, then *everything* may be said to "exist necessarily"—for everything is necessarily such that it exists if and only if it exists. So "exists necessarily" does not yield the distinction between necessary and contingent things.

A contingent thing, unlike a noncontingent thing, is a thing that might not have been—a thing that is possibly such that it came into being and is possibly such that it will pass away. And so I will return to the concepts of *coming into being* and *passing away*. (Our definitions of these concepts, like all our definitions, are in the present tense.)

D1 x is coming into being = Df x is such that there is nothing it did exemplify

D2 x has just passed away = Df Something that was such that x exists begins to be such that x does not exist

There are things that you and I *did* exemplify — say, the property of being a child — and, therefore, we are not now coming into being. And there are, I trust, properties that we *will* exemplify — say, walking somewhere later today.

If we interpret "x is such that it is F" correctly, we will see that, if a thing is *not* possibly such that it is coming into being or passing away, then it never was and never will be possibly such that it is coming into being or passing away.

The distinction between contingent and necessary things, then, is this:

D3 x is a contingent entity = Df x is possibly such that it is coming into being or has just passed away

A *necessary* thing is a thing that is not contingent.

(2) States and Individuals

Contingent things may be divided into those that are states of things and those that are not states of things. In "States and Events," we put our assumption that there *are* states of things this way:

A1 For every x, there is the state x-being-F if and only if x exemplifies being-F

Bolzano had said that a state is an entity that is *of* something. We may express this fact by saying that states are ontologically dependent upon the things of which they *are* states:

A2 For every x and y, if x is a state of y, then x is necessarily such that it is a state of y

A stone that is warm is not necessarily such that it is warm; but its-being-warm is necessarily such that it is a state of the stone.

Those contingent things that are not states of other things may be called *individual things*.

D4 x is a contingent individual = Df x is a contingent thing that is not a state

In saying that an individual thing is something that is not a state, we are saying of it that it is not "*in* a subject." But we are not assuming that "the individual alone is real," for we are assuming that there *are* states and that states are *not* individual things.

In the essay "States and Events," I have characterized *events* as constituting a subset of states.

(3) Limits and Contingent Substances

An adequate theory of categories should enable us to distinguish between those contingent individual things that may properly be called *substances* from those contingent things that are the *limits* or *boundaries* of substances.

To make this distinction, I use the locution "x is a constituent of y." I assume that the relation of being-a-constituent-of is asymmetrical and transitive: for every x and y, if x is a constituent of y, then y is not a constituent of x; and for every x, y, and z, if x is a constituent of y and if y is a constituent of z, then x is a constituent of z.

A *limit* or *boundary* is, in the following sense, a dependent individual:

D5   x is a limit (boundary) = Df (1) x is a contingent individual; and (2) every constituent of x is necessarily such that it is a constituent

Now we may say what a *contingent substance* is:

D6   x is a contingent substance = Df x is a contingent individual that is not a limit

The *parts* of a contingent substance are those of its constituents that are not boundaries or limits. It follows, therefore, that the parts of a contingent substance are themselves contingent substances. Hence, we should reject the view of Aristotle, according to which the parts of actual substances are not themselves actual substances. And we should reject the view of Leibniz, according to which actual substances cannot be parts of actual substances.

(4) Abstracta

It is often said that there is just one *ens necessarium*—namely, God. But if, as I believe, extreme realism, or Platonism, is true, and if the distinction between contingent and necessary things is to be drawn in the way that I have suggested, then it follows that there are indefinitely many necessary things. All so-called abstracta are necessary things—things incapable of coming into being or passing away. These include not only exemplified attributes, such as the attribute of being a dog, but also unexemplified attributes, such as the that of being a unicorn or that of being a round square.

Is there any reason to believe that there are abstracta that are not capable of being attributed?

What of *classes*, or *sets*? Russell showed how the principles of set theory may be construed as being principles about attributes. To say that x is a member of the class of F's is to say that x is F; to say that the class of F's includes the class of G's is to say that everything that is G is F; and more generally, to say that the class of F's is so-and-so is to say that the attribute of being-an-F is exemplified by exactly the same things as is an attribute that is so-and-so. Following Russell, then, we will say this:

D7   The class of F's is G = Df There is an attribute which is such that (a) it is G and (b) it is exemplified by all and only those things that exemplify being-F

Given that we have countenanced the being of attributes, there is no seed to assume, therefore, that *in addition to* attributes there are also such things as classes or sets. Our definition, however, enables us to use the convenient terminology of classes or sets. (Since we do not suppose that there are sets in addition to attributes, we need not face such difficult questions as: "Do sets have their members necessarily?" and "Can sets change their members?")

Aren't *states of affairs* to be counted among abstract objects? To be sure, there *is* that abstract state of affairs which is all men being mortal, as well as that state of affairs which is some men not being mortal. But we may characterize these states of affairs by reference to *being such that all men are mortal* and *being such that no men are mortal*. More generally, the state of affairs *that-p* may be characterized by reference to *being such that p*. Our definition is this:

D8   That-p is a state of affairs = Df There is an attribute which is necessarily such that it is exemplified only if p

This definition guarantees that states of affairs are abstract things and not contingent events. For attributes are necessary things and, therefore, if an attribute can be said to be "*necessarily* such that p," then the sentence replacing "p" cannot express a contingent event.

Since states of affairs are thus reducible to attributes, the expression "the state of affairs that-p *obtains*" is reducible to a statement about *exemplification*:

D9   The state of affairs that-p obtains [is true] = Df Something has an attribute which is necessarily such that it is exemplified if and only if p

What of *propositions*? If we use "proposition" to refer to a type of abstract object and not to a type of contingent thing (such as those "singular propositions" that are thought to contain contingent things as their constituents), then there would seem to be no ground for distinguishing propositions from states of affairs — unless we say that propositions are those states of affairs which are necessarily such that either they are always exemplified or they are never exemplified. And the concept of the *truth* of a proposition would be explicated by reference to exemplification in the way suggested by D9 above.

If there is reason to think that there are such things as *possible worlds*, then such entities may be identified with a certain type of state of affairs.

D10   W is a world = Df W is a state of affairs such that: for every state of affairs p, either W logically implies p or W logically implies the negation of p; and there is no state of affairs q such that W implies both q and the negation of q

In other words, a word is a self-consistent, maximal state of affairs. That it is maximal is guaranteed by the first clause of the definition; and that it is self-consistent is guaranteed by the second.

If possible worlds are thus reducible to states of affairs, and if states of affairs are reducible to attributes, then possible worlds are reducible to attributes.

What of *relations*? In contemporary logic it is usual to assimilate relations to *sets* of a certain sort — namely, those sets that are *ordered-pairs*. For example, following Kuratowski, one may construe the ordered-pair, x-paired-with-y, as the set whose sole members are (a) the set whose sole member is x and (b) the set whose sole members are x and y. Hence, we are able to distinguish the set x-paired-with-y from the set y-paired-with-x. This conception is readily carried over into the theory of attributes.

An *ordered attribute*, John-to-Mary, will be any attribute whose sole instances are: (1) an attribute whose sole instance is John and (2) an attribute whose sole instances are John and Mary. If John is, say, the tallest man in town and if John and Mary are the only people in the green Chevrolet, then an instance of the ordered attribute John-to-Mary would be the attribute of being exemplified only by the tallest man in town and by the only people in the green Chevrolet. *This* attribute, then, is one of those things that are exemplified by the relation *being taller than*. So, too, for any of the other attributes that are thus ordered from John to Mary (say, the attribute of being exemplified only by the local television repairman and by the 17th and the 284th persons to have registered in the last local election). *All* these ordered attributes exemplify the relation being-taller-than. Hence, we may say that John is paired to Mary by the relation *being taller than*.

Relations, then, will be characterized as follows:

D11 R is ordered from x to y = Df R is an attribute whose sole instances are (a) an attribute whose sole instance is x and (b) an attribute whose sole instances are x and y

D12 R is a relation = Df R is necessarily such that, if it is exemplified then there exists an x and a y such that R is ordered from x to y

This conception of relations may be extended to relations of any number of terms. If a relation has three terms, then one of its instances has two terms and the other just one; if a relation has four terms, then either (a) each of its instances has two terms or (b) one of them has three and the other just one; and so on. Every relation, no matter how many terms it has, is an *attribute* — an attribute that is exemplified by other attributes.

(5) Noncontingent Substances

We will assume, then, that there are two types of noncontingent being — those that are attributes and those that are not attributes. We will say that if there is a necessary being that is not an attribute, then it is a *necessary substance*:

D13   is a necessary substance = Df x is not contingent and x is not an attribute

A necessary substance, then, is an eternal object. And since a necessary substance is not possibly such that there is anyone who attributes it to anything, we may say with Aristotle that it is something that is "not said *of* a subject."

Such a characterization of necessary substance is essentially *negative*. We will not consider here the question whether there *is* such a being or whether, *if* there is such a being, we may characterize it in positive terms.

Index

Index

Roderick Chisholm is author of *Theory of Knowledge* (third edition, 1989), *Brentano and Intrinsic Value* (1986), *The Foundations of Knowing* (Minnesota, 1982), *The First Person* (Minnesota, 1981), *Person and Object* (1976), and *Perceiving: A Philosophical Study* (1957). He has served as president of the Eastern Division of the American Philosophical Association, of the Metaphysical Society of America, and of the International Phenomenological Society. He formerly was editor of *Philosophy and Phenomenological Research* and is professor of philosophy at Brown University. He is also the editor of numerous posthumous books by Franz Brentano.